DATE DUE

The Right to Privacy

——◆——

Adam Carlyle Breckenridge

——◆——

UNIVERSITY OF NEBRASKA PRESS · LINCOLN

Manufactured in the United States of America

Contents

———◆———

The Right to Privacy

I

A Most Comprehensive Right

———◆———

More than forty years ago in his famous dissenting opinion, U.S. Supreme Court Justice Brandeis wrote this about privacy:

> The makers of our Constitution undertook to secure conditions favorable to the pursuit of happiness.... They conferred, as against the Government, the right to be let alone—the most comprehensive of rights and the right most valued by civilized man.[1]

Privacy, in my view, is the rightful claim of the individual to determine the extent to which he wishes to share of himself with others and his control over the time, place, and circumstances to communicate to others. It means his right to withdraw or to participate as he sees fit. It is also the individual's right to control dissemination of information about himself; it is his own personal possession. As Judge Cooley observed years ago, privacy is synonymous with the right to be let alone.[2] Privacy has also been defined as a "zero-relationship" between two or more persons in the sense that there is no interaction or communication between them, if they so choose.[3]

1. *Olmstead* v. *U.S.*, 277 U.S. 438, 478 (1928).
2. Thomas M. Cooley, *A Treatise on the Law of Torts*, 2d ed. (Chicago: Callaghan & Co., 1888), p. 29.
3. Edward Shils, "Privacy: Its Constitution and Vicissitudes," *Law and Contemporary Problems* 31, no. 2, (Spring 1966): 281.

But man lives in a community of others, and he also has the
need to participate and communicate.[4] When this double-
faceted aspect of privacy is coupled with the recognized power
of government to function for the public good, there is ample
reason for much of the recent concern about invasions and
intrusions into individual privacy.[5] At issue, primarily, is the
individual's control over what of his personal affairs are
exposed without his knowledge and consent and the social
needs which run counter to it.

It has been said that the modern claim to privacy has been
based on "science, the secularization of government, and
political democracy."[6] Undoubtedly, scientific advancement
has made much of our personal privacy possible, but science
has also taken its toll in making possible severe invasions into
privacy. An example is the use of electronic devices to overhear
and record what is said without the knowledge of those speaking. Individual differences in outlook and development of personality can be attributed in part at least to the separation of
church and state. And guarantees of basic freedoms and a
respect for the dignity of man stem from the strengths of
political democracy.[7]

4. A very good analysis of social research and the relationship to
privacy is Oscar M. Ruebhausen and Orville G. Brim, Jr., "Privacy
and Behavioral Research," *Columbia Law Review* 65, no. 7 (November
1965): 1184.

5. Any claim to a *right* to privacy has ancient origins, but general
recognition of that right is relatively modern. Furthermore, governmental guarantees to protect a right to privacy are even more recent.
See Alan F. Westin, *Privacy and Freedom* (New York: Atheneum, 1967).

6. Ruebhausen and Brim, "Privacy and Behavioral Research,"
p. 1185.

7. Shils says that the respect for privacy has its roots in the "values
of modern liberalism." See his "Social Inquiry and the Autonomy
of the Individual" in Daniel Lerner, ed., *The Human Meaning of the
Social Sciences* (New York: Meridian Books, Inc., 1959), p. 120.
One writer recently observed that a wish to have privacy was closely
associated with "increased value placed on private property," and
those without property were likely to be also without privacy.
Bruno Bettelheim, "The Right to Privacy Is a Myth," *Saturday
Evening Post*, July 27, 1968, pp. 8, 9.

In recent times, however, the individual's space about him and over which he has a measure of personal control has rapidly diminished. As a nation of record keepers, we compile and maintain data about almost everyone. Many files of such information are open to public view. There is much about each of us in a manila folder in government or private offices, or other data or memory wheels ready for easy access. These data include both fact and opinion, truth and falsehood. A good deal of them accumulate without our knowledge or consent. Portions result, however, from one's own submission to questionnaires and personality tests.[8] Westin recently described three topics which involve intrusions into privacy.[9] He included what Georg Simmel called "self-invasion" or self-revelation so frequently resulting from inquiries of pollsters. A second topic is the intrusion because of curiosity, including pure gossip, but also with a generous measure of human and mechanical "peeping Toms." Third, he considers the heavy invasions into privacy by varying kinds of surveillance, such as surveillance by observation, by extraction (a psychological method), and a newer method, which he calls "reproducibility of communication." The last could be labeled general "electronic surveillance," including the use of camera devices.

The extent to which each of us has a right to determine how much of his life he must share, especially with governments, is the main topic of this study. Sooner or later it becomes the business of judges to determine the metes and bounds of individual privacy claims. Thus, it is to the decisions and opinions of judges that we must turn to find the status of claims to any right of individual privacy.[10]

8. See the careful analysis by Kenneth L. Karst, "'The Files': Legal Controls over the Accuracy and Accessibility of Stored Personal Data," *Law and Contemporary Problems*, pp. 342–376. See also, U.S. Senate, Hearings before the Subcommittee on Constitutional Rights of the Committee on the Judiciary, *Psychological Tests and Constitutional Rights*, 89th Cong., 1st sess., 1965.

9. Westin, *Privacy and Freedom*, ch. 3.

10. Most of the states have recognized varying degrees of privacy through statutes or court decisions. A few have not. The Supreme Court of Nebraska, for example, said in a 1955 case that ". . . if such

The common law did not recognize any right to privacy. Apparently, courts in the United States did not consider privacy as a *right* to be protected until the eve of the twentieth century. Since that time hundreds of cases have come before the courts to determine whether privacy exists as a legal right and, if so, then to what extent and under what conditions.

The concern about privacy may be traced, in modern times, to the famous article by Samuel D. Warren and Louis D. Brandeis which appeared in the *Harvard Law Review* in 1890, entitled, "The Right to Privacy."[11] It has been quoted or referred to in countless cases since that time.[12] The influence it has had on decisions and opinions has been unusually high, so much so that the central theme expressed has been given constitutional sanction by the U.S. Supreme Court.

One ultimately looks to the Bill of Rights of the U.S. Constitution and the interpretations given by the courts to determine the extent of one's rights to freedom of various sorts. The right to privacy, however, is not spelled out in the Constitution. The word "privacy" is not used at all. Judges, nonetheless, have considered the existence of a right to privacy since the first apparent case in 1891 in the Supreme Court of

a right is deemed necessary or desirable, such right should be provided for by action of our Legislature and not by judicial legislation on the part of our courts." *Brunson* v. *Ranks Army Store*, 161 Nebr. 519, 525. Many years ago Roscoe Pound said that if privacy was not given protection in law there was technically no legal right to privacy. *Harvard Law Review* 28, no. 4 (February 1915): 343, 363.

11. *Harvard Law Review* 4, no. 5 (December 1890): 193. (Reprinted in *Appendix*.) Their view echoed the sentiment expressed in the British Parliament by Lord Chatham, who, in a debate over the use of general warrants in 1766, is reported to have said: "The poorest man, may, in his cottage, bid defiance to all the forces of the Crown. It may be frail; its roof may shake; the wind may blow through it; the storm may enter; the rain may enter; but the King of England may not enter; all his forces dare not cross the threshold of the ruined tenement." Quoted in Thomas M. Cooley, *A Treatise on the Constitutional Limitations*, 5th ed. (Boston: Little, Brown & Co., 1883), p. 365.

12. One of the first references to the article in a higher court was in *Roberson* v. *Rochester Folding Box Co.*, 171 N.Y. 538 (1902).

New York.[13] It involved the issue whether private citizens had a right to erect a statue of a locally prominent woman over the objections of her family. It was claimed to violate privacy. In denying the claim, the Court said: "It is true that there is no reported decision which goes to this extent in maintaining the right of privacy, and in that respect this is a novel case."[14]

The first higher American court to deal with the right to privacy was in *Roberson* v. *Rochester Folding Box Co.*, a New York appellate case decided in 1902. Speaking of the lower court decision, Chief Justice Parker said:

> ... defendants had invaded what is called a "right of privacy;" in other words, the right to be let alone. Mention of such right is not to be found in Blackstone, Kent, or any other of the great commentators upon the law; nor, so far as the learning of counsel or the courts in this case have been able to discover, does its existence seem to have been asserted prior to about the year 1890, when it was presented with attractiveness, and no inconsiderable ability, in the Harvard Law Review (Volume IV, page 193).
> The so-called "right of privacy" is, as the phrase suggests, founded upon the claim that a man has the right to pass through this world, if he wills, without having his picture published, his business enterprises discussed, his successful experiments written up for the benefit of others, or his eccentricities commented upon either in hand bills or newspapers; and, necessarily, that the things which may not be written and published of him, must not be spoken of him by his neighbors, whether the comment be favorable or otherwise.[15]

13. *Schuyler* v. *Curtis*, 15 N.Y. Supp. 787 (1891). *Schuyler* may be the first to recognize the Warren-Brandeis article.

14. *Ibid.*, 788. Reference is made to the famous English case of 1849 involving Prince Albert, that it and other cases and the Warren-Brandeis article gave "... clear recognition ... of the principle that the right to which protection is given is the right to privacy." *Prince Albert* v. *Strange*, 1 Macn. & G. 25, in *Schuyler* v. *Curtis*, 789.

15. 171 N.Y., 544. Interestingly, the chief justice ignored Cooley's references to personal rights in his *Torts*, pp. 24 ff.

Three years later a Georgia court considered the question whether there was a right to privacy. The comment by Judge Cobb is of interest in tracing the development of a right to privacy because of his reference that the right is derived from natural law, a source for fundamental rights steadfastly denied by Justice Hugo Black.[16] Judge Cobb said:

> The right of privacy has its foundations in the instincts of nature. It is recognized intuitively, consciousness being witness that can be called to establish its existence. Any person whose intellect is in a normal condition recognizes at once that as to each individual member of society there are matters private and there are matters public so far as the individual is concerned. Each individual as instinctively resents any encroachment by the public upon his rights which are of a private nature as he does the withdrawal of those rights which are of a public nature. A right of privacy in matters purely private is therefore derived from natural law.[17]

Judicial pronouncements such as these provide the basic resources for both the purposes and content of this small volume. The primary object and purpose is to show how far government in the United States has gone in invading the right to personal privacy and how far government has gone also to protect that right. It is to examine how government is prevented, in the words of Justice Brandeis from obtaining "disclosure in court of what is whispered in the closet"; how government is restricted from intrusions into the privacy of the home and of the person; how the right to privacy is frequently in conflict with other claimed liberties and governmental power; and finally, to show how some invasions of privacy have become accepted as necessary in the interest of the public health, safety, morals, and the general welfare.

16. See his dissents, for example, in *Adamson* v. *California*, 322 U.S. 46, 75 (1947); and *Griswold* v. *Connecticut*, 381 U.S. 479, 511 (1965). Black has sternly insisted that any natural-law formula may not be employed to expand or contract the commands of the Bill of Rights. There is an excellent presentation of this view in Henry J. Abraham, *Freedom and the Court* (New York: Oxford Press, 1967), ch. 2.

17. *Pavesich* v. *New England Life Ins. Co.*, 122 Ga. 190, 194 (1905).

Since judges make many of these determinations in the last analysis, heavy reliance will be made on selected cases which have come before the U.S. Supreme Court. No attempt will be made to present a full development or detailed analysis of all the constitutional issues involved, nor will all facets of the concept of privacy be considered. That is not the purpose. The primary object is to present the views of judges in particular instances as a means of showing judicial attitudes toward privacy as a right and how and why and to what extent it is to be protected against governmental invasion or intrusion.

Limited attention will be given to many questions of jurisdiction, procedure, and fine points of law. And although opinions may be identified as those of the Court, or a majority, concurring, or dissenting opinion, the judicial views will include dicta without necessarily identifying them as such. As will be shown, the judicial development of the right to privacy has some of its roots in concurring and dissenting opinions. So what was "said" may be as important as what was "held" or "decided" in any particular case.

This work was prompted by recent events. During 1965 hearings were held by committees of the 89th Congress on invasions of privacy.[18] They continued into 1966. In that same year the U.S. Supreme Court handed down its decision in *Osborn* v. *U.S.* In his forceful dissent Justice Douglas summed up the fears and concerns held by many about the right to privacy.

> We are rapidly entering the age of no privacy, where everyone is open to surveillance at all times; where there are no secrets from the Government. The aggressive breaches of privacy by the Government increase with geometric proportions. Wiretapping and "bugging" run rampant, without effective judicial or legislative control.
>
> Secret observation booths in government offices and closed television circuits in industry, extending even to

18. In the House before a Subcommittee on Government Operations, and the Senate before a Subcommittee on the Judiciary.

rest rooms, are common. Offices, conference rooms, hotel rooms and even bedrooms are "bugged" for the convenience of government. Personality tests seek to ferret out a man's innermost thoughts. . . . Federal agents are often "wired" so that their conversations are either recorded on their persons or transmitted to tape recorders some blocks away. . . . They have broken and entered homes to obtain evidence. . . . The dossiers on all citizens mount in number and increase in size. Now they are being put on computers so that by pressing one button all the miserable, the sick, the suspect, the unpopular, the off-beat people of the nation can be instantly identified. These examples and many others demonstrate an alarming trend whereby the privacy and dignity of our citizens is being whittled away by sometimes imperceptible steps. Taken individually, each step may be of little consequence. But when viewed as a whole, there begins to ʾmerge a society quite unlike any we have seen—a society in which government may intrude into the secret regions of a man's life at will.[19]

During the 1967 and 1968 sessions of the Congress, the Omnibus Crime Control and Safe Streets Act was debated and passed.[20] It is a far-reaching piece of legislation which its supporters held was vital to the peace and security of the nation and which its critics roundly denounced as succumbing to the hysteria of the time.[21]

19. 385 U.S. 323, 341, 342, 343.

20. PL 90–351 of June 19, 1968. For an interesting and well-written résumé of the debate in the Congress, see Richard Harris, "Annals of Legislation," *New Yorker* magazine, December 14, 1968, p. 68. He reports that those opposing the legislation viewed it as a "piece of demagoguery."

21. During the debate on May 23, 1968, on the omnibus crime bill, Senator Edward V. Long of Missouri, with a minority of senators, sought to bring the debate into focus on the portions of the bill which deeply disturbed them. He proposed an amendment which would recognize a right to privacy. It went as follows: "The Constitution of the U.S. guarantees to all individuals a basic right of privacy. Accordingly, the Congress endorses the requirement that what an individual seeks to preserve as private is to be protected, even in an area accessible to the public. The Congress supports the view that wherever a man may be, he is entitled to know that he will

In the course of this presentation about privacy, the bias of the writer will be clear. He is strongly in favor of the maximum protection to privacy which a free society can tolerate and should ensure. He is in favor of a balance between individual rights and community interests, but with the balance tilted in favor of individual rights. Agreement is easy with Professor Beaney's statement before the *Special Inquiry on Invasion of Privacy*, held by a House subcommittee in 1965:

> You don't have to be very intelligent to see that if this drift toward more and more intrusive action by private groups and organizations of all kinds, and by Government, isn't checked, in 20 or 30 years no one will bother asking questions about privacy, and we will take it for granted that we live in a fishbowl and that we are not free men, but fish.[22]

---

remain free from unreasonable searches and seizures." On a voice vote the proposal failed! *Congressional Record*, S 6202, Amendment 717.

22. House of Representatives, Hearings before a Subcommittee of the Committee on Government Operations, 89th Cong., 1st sess., June 2, 1965, p. 15. Professor Beaney has an excellent article on privacy in the 1962 issue of *T ᵒ Supreme Court Review*, "The Constitutional Right to Privacy in the ᵤupreme Court," p. 227.

II

When Does the Constable Blunder?

On November 23, 1968, the U.S. Supreme Court agreed to hear the appeal of Ted Steven Chimel of Santa Ana, California.[1] Chimel was convicted of stealing some rare coins, and sentenced to prison. At his trial he objected to the introduction of the coins as evidence, claiming they were obtained from his home and garage without a proper search warrant.

Thus, the Court received another in a long chain of disputes over the propriety of law enforcement officers searching and seizing evidence to be used in criminal trials and in what instances those searches and seizures are within the bounds of the Fourth Amendment of the U.S. Constitution. The question is an old one. Under what conditions are officers free to comb through an individual's effects, his home, his premises, in an effort to find something which would support an arrest and later a conviction for violation of law? The question squarely is whether a man's home is out of bounds to those whom he chooses to deny entry. It is a matter of a right to privacy.

Among the great tasks of a free society is finding and observing that delicate balance between the rights of the individual to be free from interference by government and the needs of

1. *People* v. *Chimel*, 439 P 2d 333 (1968). On June 23, 1969, the Court decided in favor of Chimel.

that society to protect itself and its members from those who commit defined wrongs. It is also a task of drawing a line defending the rights of the individual and at the same time not having his exercise of rights interfere with the rights of others.

Undoubtedly the change in the United States from a predominately rural to an urban society has increased the concern about rights and rights in conflict. In our homes and where we work, in our automobiles and in going to and from places of whatever nature, we are in very close proximity to others. Any movement of activity by any one of us may affect adversely the actions of someone else. What one of us does in the exercise of freedom may be claimed to interfere with the freedom of another. What bothers one person may be of little or no consequence to another. Some people find governmental regulations no serious · inconvenience and applaud their enforcement. Others in similar circumstances rebel against them, violate them, and, if caught and convicted, denounce them as contrary to their guaranteed rights.

The recent history of individual rights and freedom shows reasons for concern about their protection and extension. Intrusions and interferences by officials of government into the daily lives of people have risen in recent decades. Whether this comes as a result of the nearness of living with thousands of others in a small geographical area and has made more rules necessary to promote a particular kind of society, or both, is not easily determined. But even in a heavily populated area most people want and insist upon some degree of privacy notwithstanding the claim that in an urban society one does not know or care about his neighbors.

In his dissent in *U.S.* v. *On Lee*, Circuit Judge Jerome Frank had this to say:

> . . . the "sanctity of a man's house and the privacies of life" still remain protected from the uninvited intrusion of physical means by which words within the house are secretly communicated to a person on the outside. A man can still control part of his environment, his house; he can retreat thence from outsiders, secure in the knowledge

that they cannot get at him without disobeying the Constitution. That is still a sizeable hunk of liberty—worth protecting from encroachment. A sane, decent, civilized society must provide some such oasis, some shelter from public scrutiny, some insulated enclosure, some enclave, some inviolate place which is a man's castle.[2]

In writing opinions, judges of U.S. and state courts frequently make reference to the English case of *Entick* v. *Carrington*,[3] decided prior to the Revolutionary War. In that case the use of "general" warrants was disallowed with the declaration that "by the laws of England every invasion of private property, be it ever so minute, is a trespass."[4]

The use of general warrants was known during American colonial times when British customs agents searched homes for smuggled goods. Memory of those abuses gave impetus to the Fourth Amendment to the U.S. Constitution.

The rights of the people to be secure in their persons, houses, papers, and effects, against unreasonable searches and seizures, shall not be violated, and no warrants shall issue, but upon probable cause supported by oath or affirmation, and particularly describing the place to be searched, and the persons or things to be seized.

Thus, there is a right to privacy of person, house, papers, and effects. But it is not a right without limitations. The limitations are several, but the intruding arm of government can be extended if the action is not unreasonable. Unless some actions by some people did not have to be controlled, there would be no need for searches and seizures. And conversely, if there were not searches and seizures which are claimed to be unreasonable, there would be little opportunity for contest about the words or the purposes of the Fourth Amendment. The opposite, of course, is also true. Lawyers and judges and scholars have written thousands of words in

2. 193 F 2d 306, 315, 316 (1951).
3. 19 St. Tr. 1029, K & L. 174 (1765).
4. Cited in *Boyd* v. *U.S.*, 116 U.S. 616, 627 (1886).

debate and judgment and analysis over the exercise of law enforcement within the meaning of that amendment.

The modern period on the right to privacy by route of the Fourth Amendment stems from efforts to enforce the Eighteenth Amendment and from comparatively recent developments in technology. But the U.S. Supreme Court had the first occasion to interpret the Fourth Amendment in 1886. A warrant to search and seize evidence to be used in a criminal trial had to "particularly describe" that which was sought. That decision more than eighty years ago also related the Fourth and Fifth Amendments making a search unreasonable if it would result in self-incrimination.

For the last forty years, debate has ranged far and wide over whether evidence obtained by listening to or recording conversations made by a telephone come within the purview of the restraints of the Fourth and Fifth Amendments. This had its formal judicial beginnings in the celebrated case of *Olmstead* v. *U.S.*, decided in 1928.[5]

The issue was whether evidence given in court obtained by tapping a telephone line violated the protections guaranteed by the Fourth and Fifth Amendments. Is a telephone conversation private and beyond the would-be intruder? And how does "conversation" fit into the words of the Fourth Amendment?

The Fourth Amendment does not prohibit any such invasion of privacy. It prevents only intrusions which are unreasonable. In the majority opinion for the U.S. Supreme Court in *Olmstead*, Chief Justice Taft said that the well-known historical purpose of the Fourth Amendment was "to prevent the use of governmental force to search a man's house, his person, his papers and his effects; and to prevent their seizure against his will." He said that the search had to be for *material* things. Citing some earlier cases, he found that none of them hold the Fourth Amendment is violated ". . . unless there has been

5. 277 U.S. 438. It was specifically overruled in 1967. It is too early to do more than speculate on the effects of the authorization for wiretapping by the Omnibus Crime Control and Safe Streets Act of 1968.

an official search and seizure of his person, or such a seizure of his papers or his tangible effects, or an actual physical invasion of his house . . . for purpose of making a seizure."[6]

Taft denied there had been an improper search and seizure, for there had been no physical entry into a private dwelling. (The tapping had been done elsewhere, even in violation of a state law.) He commented that Congress could declare evidence obtained by wiretapping inadmissible, but "the Courts may not adopt such a policy by attributing an enlarged and unusual meaning to the Fourth Amendment."[7]

Justices Brandeis and Holmes dissented from the Taft opinion. The dissenting opinions gave forceful arguments against wiretapping. Justice Brandeis wrote:

> The makers of our Constitution undertook to secure conditions favorable to the pursuit of happiness. They recognized the significance of man's spiritual nature, of his feelings and of his intellect. They knew that only a part of the pain, pleasure, and satisfactions of life are to be found in material things. They sought to protect Americans in their beliefs, their thoughts, their emotions and their sensations. They conferred, as against the Government, *the right to be let alone—the most comprehensive of rights and the right most valued by civilized man*. To protect that right, every unjustifiable intrusion by the Government upon the privacy of the individual, whatever the means employed, must be deemed a violation of the Fourth Amendment. . . . Discovery and invention have made it possible for the Government, by means far more effective than stretching upon the rack, to obtain disclosure in court of what is whispered in the closet.[8]

Those views were sounded again and again through the years which followed, and the Taft position was finally eroded away when the Supreme Court specifically overruled it in the 1967 case of *Katz* v. *U.S.*[9]

What is a proper search and seizure? The following conditions appear to be required: A warrant must be issued by a

6. *Ibid.*, 463, 466.
7. *Ibid.*, 466.
8. *Ibid.*, 478, 473. Emphasis supplied.
9. 389 U.S. 347 (1967).

magistrate or other official authorized to do so; it must specify the place or places to be searched; it must specify the person or persons to be searched and set forth the purpose; it must specify the thing or things to be seized; it must be dated and time limits set on the duration of the warrant; and it cannot be issued except on probable cause that the search will yield specific evidence for use in a criminal prosecution.

When a person is arrested with a warrant, the arresting officer can usually search his person, especially if he is seeking a dangerous weapon or stolen goods. If an individual is arrested without a warrant a search is valid only if the arrest is valid. The issue centers upon how far the search can proceed if there is no warrant to search. A search of premises without a search warrant, for example, cannot be done if the arrest did not take place there.[10]

In the *Boyd* case of 1886, the U.S. Supreme Court was concerned with the "intimate relation between" the Fourth and Fifth Amendments and found that they "run almost into each other . . . ." Commenting upon the issues involved in a disavowal of general search warrants, Justice Bradley wrote: "It is not the breaking of his doors, and the rummaging of his drawers, that constitutes the essence of the offense; but it is the invasion of his indefeasible right of personal security, personal liberty and private property . . . ."[11]

In *Boyd* the defendant did not produce certain papers under his control. He was in the position that if he did not produce them the presumption would be made that the allegations against him were valid. And if he did produce them they would be used against him for whatever they contained. It was a case of having the prosecution tell him: "Heads I win; tails you lose!" The Court found that a requirement that the

10. State laws on the subject of search and seizure are not identical, and no attempt will be made to detail those variations. In some, only stolen property, weapons, and gambling devices can be seized under the search of a person without a warrant. See also, *Dickinson Law Review* 73, no. 1 (Fall 1968). The issue emphasizes the subject of warrants and search.

11. 116 U.S. 616, 630.

papers be produced was not only the same as search and seizure, but that it would also constitute an unreasonable search and seizure, making the defendant a "witness against himself."

The Fifth Amendment provides:

> No person shall be held to answer for a capital, or other-wise infamous crime, unless on a presentment or indict-ment of a Grand Jury, except in cases arising in the land or naval forces, or in the Militia, when in actual service in time of War or public danger; nor shall any person be subject for the same offence to be twice put in jeop-ardy of life or limb; nor shall be compelled in any criminal case to be a witness against himself, nor be deprived of life, liberty, or property, without due process of law; nor shall private property be taken for public use, without just compensation.

The significant words are "no person shall be compelled in any criminal case to be a witness against himself, nor be deprived of life, liberty, or property, without due process of law."

Some years after Prohibition had been repealed and Mr. Olmstead's plight was likely forgotten, the U.S. Supreme Court had occasion to consider another governmental use of advanced technology. It also involved eavesdropping and without the knowledge and consent of those conversing. But in this case no wires were tapped. This was *Goldman* v. *U.S.*, decided in 1942.[12]

Federal agents placed a dictaphone device on the adjoining wall and were able to listen to conversations in the room on the other side. There was no penetration of the wall. There was no object within the premises of those whose talks were being overheard. The microphone was sensitive enough to pick up the conversations, the wall notwithstanding.

The majority of the Court thought there was no unlawful entry, no violation of privacy, no violation of the Federal Communications Act of 1934 which prohibited the use of

12. 316 U.S. 129.

evidence gained from wiretapping. This was not wiretapping! They ignored the eloquence of Justice Holmes in his dissent in *Olmstead*. Holmes wrote:

> It is desirable that criminals should be detected, and to that end that all available evidence should be used. It also is desirable that the Government should not itself foster and pay for other crimes, when they are the means by which the evidence is to be obtained. If it pays its officers for having got evidence by crime I do not see why it may not as well pay them for getting it in the same way, and I can attach no importance to protestations of disapproval if it knowingly accepts and pays and announces that in the future it will pay for the fruits. We have to choose, and for my part I think it is a less evil that some criminals should escape than that the Government should play an ignoble part.[13]

Listening devices of varying types were easily obtained and preventing their use was not then—nor since—a simple task. It is the use of evidence so obtained which is the basis of controversy. Justice Murphy's dissent in *Goldman* is useful to note, not only because of the argument he presented, but because his views were used ultimately in majority opinions. To Murphy it was clear that the detectaphone was used to permit an unreasonable search and seizure. "One of the great boons secured to the inhabitants of this country by the Bill of Rights is the right of personal privacy guaranteed by the Fourth Amendment. In numerous ways the law protects the individual against unwarranted intrusions by others into his private affairs."[14] The Fourth Amendment, wrote Murphy, puts a restraint on the arm of the government and prevents it from invading the sanctity of the home or "his private quarters" except under the safeguards intended to prevent oppression and the abuse of the authority of government. He found comfort in the Brandeis dissent in *Olmstead*. He thought that man's spiritual freedom depended upon the preservation of the right to privacy. His argument continued:

13. 277 U.S. 438, 470.
14. 316 U.S. 129, 136.

There was no physical entry in this case. But the search of one's home or office no longer requires physical entry, for science has brought forth far more effective devices for the invasion of the person's privacy than the direct and obvious methods of oppression which were detested by our forebears and which inspired the Fourth Amendment. Surely the spirit motivating the framers of that Amendment would abhor these new devices no less. Physical entry may be wholly immaterial. Whether the search of private quarters is accomplished by placing on the outer walls . . . a detectaphone that transmits to the outside listener the intimate details of a private conversation, or by new methods of photography that will penetrate walls or overcome distances, the privacy of the citizen is equally invaded by agents of the Government and intimate personal matters are laid bare to view.[15]

It was not the invasion, as such, which bothered Murphy. Rather it was that the invasion was not conducted in harmony with the requirements of the Fourth Amendment.

As forewarned by Brandeis and others, science and technology continued to permit movement by silence and stealth, unobserved. Volume 343 of the U.S. Supreme Court Reports gives one such case.

In *On Lee* v. *U.S.*,[16] an acquaintance of On Lee was in the employ of the U.S. government working on narcotics violations, but this relationship was not known by On Lee. The agent had a radio transmitter concealed in his coat pocket and an antenna concealed in the sleeve. Any conversation carried on between the agent and On Lee was then broadcast to a receiver carried by a second agent not far from the laundry of On Lee where the conversations occurred and some incriminating evidence obtained.

At the trial, On Lee maintained that his rights had been violated, that his privacy had been invaded. (Agent number one did not appear to testify.) Justice Jackson gave the decision for the Court. To him there was no unreasonable search and no need for a warrant, no need to let On Lee know that his conversation was being recorded for use against him. He used

15. *Ibid.*, 139.
16. 343 U.S. 747 (1952).

the decision in *Goldman*, involving the detectaphone, to support his position. Jackson maintained that the agent entered the premises of On Lee with his consent or at least with his implied consent or invitation. The agent did not force his way into the laundry and On Lee did not submit to the force of any authority. There would be no objection for misconduct by the government's agent that On Lee talked indiscreetly. That was no different from having someone use bifocals, field glasses, or a telescope to magnify what could not otherwise be seen. Such uses, Jackson wrote, were not illegal. The same results might have been obtained if the spoken word had been overheard through an open window.

Justice Frankfurter did not approve. He was apprehensive about the future directions such sanctions would take. "Ways," he wrote, "may some day be developed" which would permit the government to copy papers and reproduce them in court without moving them and thereby expose in court the "most intimate occurrences of the home." [17] He speculated that scientific advances might one day bring means of exploring unexpressed thoughts, beliefs, and emotions.

Justice Burton also dissented, but his primary concern was that a proper line always was being drawn, as cases arose, between the need to seek out the criminal but also to protect the rights which were guaranteed. He thought the majority went too far. [18]

The justices may not be masters of the science of technology but they understood the uses to which that technology may be put to thwart the restrictions against invasions of privacy. *Silverman* v. *U.S.* is a case in point. [19] In this case a "spike mike" was put into a wall so that officers could overhear conversations, and some of the information gained was found to be incriminating. There was no warrant to search or seize.

The majority of the U.S. Supreme Court thought this was an unwarranted invasion of privacy. The spike made contact with the heating system ductwork of the house and thus

17. *Ibid.*, 759.
18. *Ibid.*, 765.
19. 365 U.S. 505 (1961).

became a conductor of sound from the entire house. Conversations taking place on both floors were audible to the officers next door and their testimony was admitted at a trial. Speaking for the majority, Justice Stewart found this intrusion "beyond the pale" of prior court decisions in which a "closely divided court" had held that eavesdropping accomplished by other electronic means did not amount to an invasion of the rights guaranteed by the Fourth Amendment. He especially quoted *On Lee* and *Goldman*, indicating that the Court had taken special pains to show that there had been no "physical" trespass in either case. He declined to go beyond the prescription in *Goldman* by "even a fraction of an inch."

But these fine distinctions were too much for Justice Douglas. A device used to overhear which was placed only "on" the wall is permissible but to penetrate a wall not in the view of anyone being overheard as an invasion of privacy was a distinction too fine for him. He thought the invasion of privacy was present in both cases.

"Was not the wrong in both cases done when the intimacies of the home were tapped, recorded, or revealed?" To Douglas the depth of the penetration of the electronic device "is not the measure of the injury." There was a search in *Goldman* and *Silverman* and a warrant was required by the Constitution. Douglas thought these cases should not turn on the kind of electronic equipment used but "rather our sole concern should be whether the privacy of the home was invaded. Since it was invaded here, and since there was no search warrant obtained as required . . ." there was reason to set the convictions aside.[20]

For nearly four decades wiretapping had a degree of protection from the U.S. Supreme Court. Taft's words in *Olmstead* prevailed until 1967.[21] Taft had written: "We think, therefore, that the wiretapping here disclosed did not amount to a search or seizure within the meaning of the Fourth Amendment."[22] The conversation was overheard away from

20. *Ibid.*, 512, 513.
21. *Katz* v. *U.S.*, 389 U.S. 347.
22. 277 U.S. 438, 466.

the premises. There were no papers or effects seized. And the difference to Taft was that papers and effects meant tangible things and only words were used against Olmstead. There was no physical intrusion, no trespass. But gradually the words of Justice Brandeis were to prevail. "Subtler and more far-reaching means of invading privacy have become available to the Government." [23]

During the period after *Olmstead* many cases came before the U.S. Supreme Court and other courts involving the admissibility of evidence obtained from various types of eavesdropping devices. The problem was how to fit the use within the rules involving legal search, seizure, and trespass. Two 1967 cases are of special interest. One, a New York case,[24] held that a state statute was defective since it left too much discretion to the officer executing the authority to carry out the eavesdropping, that it did not require prompt use, had no termination date, and permitted unconsented entry without a "showing of exigent circumstances."

As abhorrent as eavesdropping may be, law enforcement officers in substantial numbers insist that eavesdropping in whatever form is essential to effective crime control. But in *Berger* there is the suggestion that all kinds of electronic surveillance must be restricted in the interest of the right to individual privacy. Having so stated, it is evident that the justices of the high court are aware of the very strong criticisms made of their decisions and sometimes their reactions enter their opinions.

In *Berger*, Justice Clark said: "It is said that neither a warrant nor a statute authorizing eavesdropping can be drawn so as to meet the Fourth Amendment's requirements. If that be true then the 'fruits' of eavesdropping devices are barred under the Amendment." But he did not find this to be the case. He cited examples of the Court's approval of eavesdropping under "specific conditions and circumstances." The New York statute did not meet those conditions and circumstances by its "obvious" defects. Clark noted that the

23. *Ibid.*, 473.
24. *Berger* v. *N.Y.*, 388 U.S. 41 (1967).

Court had sanctioned eavesdropping in *Goldman*, *Lee*, and *Osborn*. In *Osborn*, a 1966 case, the eavesdropping device was permitted where the "commission of a specific offense" was charged, and its use was "under the most precise and discriminating circumstances" and the "effective administration of justice" was at stake.[25]

In the second 1967 case, the Court reviewed claims about possible confusion between what would and what would not be permitted through eavesdropping. In *Katz* v. *U.S.*, Justice Stewart wrote:

> . . . the Fourth Amendment cannot be translated into a general constitutional "right to privacy." That Amendment protects individual privacy against certain kinds of governmental intrusion, but its protections go no further, and often have nothing to do with privacy at all. Other provisions of the Constitution protect personal privacy from other forms of governmental invasion. But the protection of a person's *general* right to privacy— his right to be let alone by other people—is, like the protection of his property and of his very life, left largely to the law of the individual States.[26]

In *Katz* the FBI placed a "bug" on the outside wall of an outdoor public telephone booth. In the trial the government stressed the fact that the telephone booth was constructed partly of glass and anyone in it could be observed easily from the outside. But Justice Stewart said of that:

> . . . what he sought to exclude when he entered the booth was not the intruding eye—it was the uninvited ear. . . . One who occupies it, shuts the door behind him, and pays the toll that permits him to place a call, is surely entitled to assume that the words will not be broadcast to the world.

At that point the ax fell on the Taft decision in *Olmstead*.

> We conclude that the underpinnings of *Olmstead* and *Goldman* have been so eroded by our subsequent decisions that the "trespass" doctrine there enunciated can no

25. *Ibid.*, 63.
26. 389 U.S., 350, 351.

longer be regarded as controlling. The Government's activities in electronically listening to and recording the petitioner's words violated the privacy upon which he justifiably relied while using the telephone booth and thus constituted a "search and seizure" within the meaning of the Fourth Amendment. The fact that the electronic device employed to achieve that end did not happen to penetrate the wall of the booth can have no constitutional significance.[27]

A year later, in 1968, the Court had occasion to deal with wiretapping and the admissibility of evidence obtained in a *state* court.

In the summer of 1963, Clyde Franklin Lee ordered the installation of a telephone in his home near Orlando, Florida. He was advised by the telephone company that no private line was available but the necessary installation was made on a four-party line. A week later, in a nearby house, the Orlando police had the telephone company install a telephone on the same party line. Later the police attached an automatic

27. *Ibid.*, 352, 353. The decision in *Katz* was based only on the Fourth Amendment. The omnibus crime act of 1968 may clash with that decision as a result of the use of electronic surveillance which Attorney General Mitchell says he has authorized. Former Attorney General Clark would not authorize wiretapping and similar "bugging" authority except in national security cases. Mitchell has also been quoted as saying he would continue that practice begun by his predecessor, but also extend it to "organized crimes and other major crimes." These were not identified further. *New York Times*, January 15, 1969, pp. 1, 22.

On March 24, 1969, the U.S. Supreme Court decided *Desist* v. *U.S.* involving the use of tape recordings made by federal officers in a room adjoining that of the defendants, but without physically intruding the latter's room. The Court would not overturn the conviction—involving a conspiracy to import and conceal heroin in violation of the narcotics laws—nor make a ruling that it would be retroactive following *Katz*. "Exclusion of electronic eavesdropping evidence seized before *Katz* would increase the burden on the administration of justice, would overturn convictions based on fair reliance upon pre-*Katz* decisions, and would not serve to deter similar searches and seizures in the future." The rule in *Katz* was to apply in cases after December 18, 1967.

actuator to the telephone in the second house, as well as a tape recorder and a set of earphones. The equipment was connected so that all of Lee's incoming and outgoing calls could be recorded without the telltale click of the police-installed receiver or of any noises which might otherwise be transmitted had the receiver been removed in the ordinary manner. In due course, the police obtained some incriminating information.

At Lee's trial, evidence obtained via the recorder was introduced over Lee's objection. The U.S. Supreme Court sustained him. It found that there "clearly *is* a Federal statute applicable in Florida and every other state that made illegal the conduct of the Orlando authorities . . ." and the conversations so obtained were inadmissible as evidence in the Florida court.[28] It violated Section 605 of the FCC Act. A footnote in the opinion bears quoting.

> A party-line user's privacy is obviously vulnerable, but it does not necessarily follow that his telephone conversations are completely unprotected by Section 605. In many areas of the country private telephone lines are not available; in other areas they are available only at higher rates than party-lines. There is nothing in the language or history of Section 605 to indicate that Congress meant to afford any less protection to those who, by virtue of geography or financial hardship, must use party-line telephones.[29]

The Court then proceeded to scold law enforcement officers throughout the entire United States.

> The hope was expressed in *Schwartz* v. *Texas* that "enforcement of the statutory prohibition in Section 605 can be achieved under the penal provisions" of the Communications Act. That has proved to be a vain hope. Research has failed to uncover a single reported prosecution of a law enforcement officer for violation of Section 605 since the section was enacted.[30]

28. *Lee* v. *Florida*, 392 U.S. 378 (1968).
29. *Ibid*, 381.
30. *Ibid*, 386.

The use of electronic devices for "bugging" or eaves-dropping received strong sanction from the 90th Congress with the passage of the Omnibus Crime Control and Safe Streets Act of 1968. It was passed on June 19, 1968. Title III gives wide authority to federal and state authorities to intercept "written and oral" communications. Although the extent to which it will be used remains to be seen, the Nixon administration indicated early in 1969 that the authority given by the statute would be employed. How far it will make inroads into the line of decisions presented above is also an unknown. It should be remembered that the Supreme Court relied heavily on Section 605 of the FCC Act which prohibited the introduction of evidence obtained by wiretapping. Message interception as noted, however, was acceptable under specific conditions and circumstances, and where there was a specific offense involved and when done under the most precise and discriminating circumstances or when the effective administration of justice "in a federal court was at stake."

With the passage of the 1968 crime act, the U.S. Supreme Court undoubtedly will soon face claims against electronic surveillance, but it will have different statutory ground rules than those previously relied upon. Even so, the broad authority granted in the act may mean invasion of rights and be abusively used. Opponents of the act made strong representations against it during congressional debate. They claimed it would be illegal and contrary to the Fourth and Fifth Amendments because of its very broad provisions.[31]

31. Of interest are the "Congressional Findings" relating to the act.

Organized criminals make extensive use of wire and oral communications in their criminal activities. The interception of such communications to obtain evidence of the commission of crimes or to prevent their commission is an indispensable aid to law enforcement and the administration of justice.

To safeguard the privacy of innocent persons, the interception of wire and oral communications where none of the parties to the communication has consented to the interception should be allowed only when authorized by a court of competent jurisdiction and should remain under the control and supervision of the authorizing court. Interception of wire and oral communications

On March 10, 1969, the U.S. Supreme Court decided some national security cases involving the alleged illegal use of eavesdropping devices. The convictions were for violations of the U.S. Code for conspiring to transmit to the Soviet Union information relating to the national defense of the United States and related violations.[32] The Court said that the exclusionary rule fashioned in the *Weeks* and *Mapp* cases excluded any evidence in a criminal trial which was seized from a defendant in violation of his Fourth Amendment rights. The government sought to bypass that rule as "no overheard conversation is arguably relevant to this prosecution."

The majority opinion did not accept a deviation from former rulings, but the Court was mindful of Title III of the omnibus crime act. Justice White wrote:

> The security of persons and property remains a fundamental value which law enforcement officers must accept. Nor should those who flaunt the rules escape unscathed. In this respect we are mindful that there is now a comprehensive statute making unauthorized electronic surveillance a serious crime. The general rule under the statute is that official eavesdropping and wiretapping are permitted only with probable cause and a warrant. Without experience showing the contrary, we should not assume that this new statute will be cavalierly disregarded or will not be enforced against transgressors.

White did not make reference to the provision in the statute that permits so-called emergency eavesdropping without any approval from a magistrate. In any event, the convictions were vacated and remanded. It was not surprising, therefore,

---

should be limited to certain major types of offenses and specific categories of crime with assurances that the interception is justified and that the information obtained thereby will not be misused.

Of interest is the *Congressional Record* for May 22, 1968, S 6095–6113, and May 23, 1968, S 6201–6246. The act also established a fifteen-member National Commission for the Review of Federal and State Laws Related to Wiretapping and Electronic Surveillance.

32. *Alderman* v. *U.S.*, ———— U.S. ————; *Ivanov* v. *U.S.*, ———— U.S. ————; and *Butenko* v. *U.S.*, ———— U.S. ————.

that strong representations opposing the decision would be forthcoming. These came almost immediately from the Department of Justice. Officials there were reported to have been "stunned" about the ruling, claiming among other things that the government would have to abandon many prosecutions. [33] In his opinion, White said that the evidence so obtained could not be restricted to screening only *in camera*, but had to be available to the defendant. He went further:

> The Government concedes that it must disclose to petitioners any surveillance records which are relevant to the decision of this ultimate issue. And it recognizes that this disclosure must be made even though attended by potential danger to the reputation or safety of third parties or to the national security—unless the United States would prefer dismissal of the case to disclosure of the information.

The reference to the potential danger to the reputation of the United States was an acknowledgment that the government tapped telephones of foreign embassies. Apparently such practices were long-standing and would be known at least to Justices White and Marshall by reason of their prior service in the Department of Justice.

The majority opinion contained two significant explanations about the possible adverse impact to the government. One was that "it must be remembered that disclosure will be limited to the transcripts of petitioner's own conversations and of those which took place on his premises." This was a repetition made earlier in the opinion that violations of electronic surveillance restrictions "would occur if the United States unlawfully overheard conversations of a petitioner himself or conversations occurring on his premises, whether or not he was present or participated in those conversations." This apparently was in anticipation of the objections by the Department of Justice and other critics of the Court's opinion. Two weeks later the Court refused to rehear the case. Of interest, however, was the caustic comment by Justice Stewart about

33. *New York Times*, March 12, 1969, pp. 1, 28; *National Observer*, March 17, 1969, p. 4.

criticism of the opinion. He said that a careful reading of the opinion would show that the Court had not excluded the government from surveillance in search of foreign intelligence.

> One might suppose that all of this should be entirely clear to any careful reader of the Court's opinion, but 10 years of experience here have taught me that the most carefully written opinions are not always carefully read— even by those most directly concerned.[34]

Foreign embassies seemed to be out of the bounds of protection from the restrictions. White had tried to make this clear, saying in the majority opinion that "none of this means that any petitioner will have an unlimited license to rummage in the files of the Department of Justice." Nonetheless, reports highlighted the impression from Stewart's comment that the Court would ease the bugging restrictions, and companion reports indicated expressions of relief by government lawyers —apparently not too ruffled by Stewart's comments.[35]

The Fourth Amendment places emphasis upon the freedom of the individual against having unreasonable searches and seizures involving his person, his premises, his papers, and his effects. These represent tangible things rather than the more vexing question of conversations which are quite intangible. Arrests with or without warrants and searches and seizures with or without warrants make up the greatest number of privacy invasions.

Several years ago in seeking some fugitives from justice, the FBI kept a cabin in California under surveillance. They obtained a warrant for the arrest of two men, but there was no warrant for the search of the cabin or the taking of any of its contents. In due course, two men were arrested—those named in the warrant. But two other men, inside the cabin, were also arrested, but without a warrant. A search was then made of the cabin and the entire contents removed and taken to an FBI laboratory some distance away.

34. *National Observer*, March 31, 1969, p. 3.
35. *Ibid.*

The U.S. Supreme Court in *Kremen* v. *U.S.*[36] found the search unlawful. There was no search warrant, and the men named in the arrest warrant were outside, not inside, the cabin. As if to magnify the situation, the printed opinion included an itemized list of the contents of the cabin which fills, in fine print, pages 349 to 359 of that volume of the U.S. Reports.

In *Harris* v. *U.S.*,[37] a 1947 case, a different quality is given to a claimed illegal search. The Court upheld the search as proper and not an unwarranted invasion of privacy. The accused was arrested with a warrant in his apartment. After making the arrest the officers made an intensive five-hour search of the apartment. In the bottom drawer in the bedroom they found an envelope marked "personal papers." It was opened and found to contain stolen draft cards, possession of which was a violation of the U.S. Code.

In the majority opinion, it was pointed out that only unreasonable searches and seizures are within the constitutional interdict and that each case had to be decided on its own facts and circumstances.

> The Fourth Amendment has never been held to require that every valid search and seizure be effected under the authority of a search warrant. Search and seizure incident to lawful arrest is a practice of ancient origin and has long been an integral part of law-enforcement procedures of the U.S. and of the individual states.[38]

But in this case the agents entered the apartment under the authority of a lawful warrant for arrest. And in the course of a valid search the agents came upon property of the United States which was in the illegal possession of the petitioner. It was the property "of which the government was entitled to possession."

36. 353 U.S. 346 (1956). Among the items taken from the cabin included: one dishrag; one pair socks—men's gray—dirty; one toothbrush; one flashlight bulb; one clove garlic; one roll toilet paper.

37. 331 U.S. 145.

38. *Ibid.*, 150, 151.

Was the time-consuming search of an apartment, lasting five hours, a search incident to arrest, or was it acceptable seizure because the time spent uncovered property of the government? Justice Frankfurter, with support from Justices Murphy and Rutledge would not let the nice distinction pass without protest. Frankfurter wrote:

> Because I deem the implications of the Court's decision to have serious threats to basic liberties, I consider it important to underscore my concern over the outcome . . . permits rummaging throughout a house without a search warrant on the ostensible grounds of looking for the instruments of a crime for which an arrest, but only an arrest, has been authorized.[39]

He then suggested a possible status for the right to privacy in relation to other rights.

> Freedom of speech, of the press, of religion, easily summon powerful support against encroachment. The prohibition against unreasonable search and seizure is normally invoked by those accused of crime, and criminals have few friends. The implications of such encroachment, however, reach far beyond the thief or the black marketeer. I cannot give legal sanction to what was done in this case.[40]

Frankfurter's position later prevailed. On June 23, 1969, the last day of the Warren court, the majority opinion was overruled in the case of *Chimel* v. *California*.

But Frankfurter had no trouble in sanctioning seizure after an arrest in a hotel room in a 1960 case.[41] After the accused had checked out of his hotel room following the arrest, the FBI searched the room with the permission of the hotel management and found some incriminating evidence, some of which was in a wastebasket. The court opinion sustained the search without a search warrant on the finding that the evidence was abandoned by the defendant and therefore not affected

39. *Ibid.*, 155, 156.
40. *Ibid.*, 156.
41. *Abel* v. *U.S.*, 362 U.S. 217 (1960). Abel was suspected of being a notorious Soviet spy.

by any rights involving rules of search and seizure. The items introduced in evidence were found after the defendant had checked out and paid his hotel bill. They were where "petitioner had put them while packing his belongings preparing to leave." There was no pretense that the search by the FBI was for any purpose other than to gather evidence of crime, in this case espionage. As Frankfurter put it, it was entirely lawful, even· without a warrant, for the room had been vacated and the property abandoned. Was it proper to seize the entire contents of the wastebasket even though some of the items had no connection with any crime? "So far as the record shows, petitioner had abandoned these items. He had thrown them away." [42] Frankfurter concluded that it was not unlawful for the government to take property which had been abandoned.

A 1958 decision involving search and seizure is related to the enforcement of the revenue stamp requirements under the liquor laws.[43] It differs from others presented thus far in that no electronic device was used and an arrest and a search and seizure was made even though there was adequate time to obtain a warrant.

Officers were reported to have a farmhouse in Georgia under observation, believing it contained an illicit distillery. A daytime search warrant was requested and authorized. The farmhouse was kept under surveillance until after dark. The warrant was not used. The officers then observed that strong evidence in view supported the belief about the distillery. After dark, the officers forced their way into the house and without arresting anyone seized certain distilling equipment found in the dwelling. The householder was away at the time, but upon his return about an hour following the forced entry, he was arrested.

The U.S. Supreme Court found that the seizure violated the Fourth Amendment. The opinion stated that the purpose was to search and seize, during daylight, and to arrest. "It is settled doctrine that probable cause for belief that certain

42. *Ibid.*, 241.
43. *Jones* v. *U.S.*, 357 U.S. 493.

articles subject to seizure are in a dwelling cannot of itself justify a search without a warrant."[44] Otherwise, protections would be largely nullified. That indicated lack of authority for a reasonable search. There was time to have obtained a valid warrant, but apparently no effort was made to obtain a new one to correct the passage of time from daylight to darkness. The evidence so seized could not be used against the defendant.

A similar situation arose from the *Johnson* case.[45] Here a federal narcotics agent detected the odor of burning opium coming from a hotel room, and without a warrant, entered and searched the room, found opium and smoking apparatus, and arrested the occupant. He was later convicted. The agent had been tipped off by a local police officer who had received the information from a known narcotics user. The defendant, Johnson, had challenged the introduction of the evidence as an illegal search and seizure. He also claimed that there was no ground for obtaining a search warrant if one had been sought.

The U.S. Supreme Court agreed in part, but not enough to sustain both claims. There was time, the opinion stated, for the agent to seek a search warrant, but he did not do so; therefore the search was illegal, and only from the illegal search did the agent find out who was committing a crime.

> If the presence of odors is testified to before a magistrate and he finds the affiant qualified to know the odor, and it is one sufficiently distinctive to identify a forbidden substance, this Court has never held such a basis insufficient to justify issuance of a search warrant. Indeed it might very well be found to be evidence of most persuasive character.[46]

The justice then supported the need for privacy, but also gave recognition to society's claim that crime is committed in private and must be reckoned with.

44. Citing *Agnello* v. *U.S.*, 269 U.S. 20 (1925), 497.
45. *Johnson* v. *U.S.*, 333 U.S. 10 (1948).
46. *Ibid.*, 13.

Crime, even in the privacy of one's own quarters, is, of course, of grave concern to society, and the law allows such crime to be reached on proper showing. The right of officers to thrust themselves into a home is also a grave concern, not only to the individual but to a society which chooses to dwell in reasonable security and freedom from surveillance. When the right of privacy must reasonably yield to the right of search is, as a rule, to be decided by a judicial officer, not by a policeman or governmental agent.[47]

These cases illustrate the dilemma faced by judges and also those not so directly involved. In some, a warrant might have been difficult to obtain. In others, seeking a warrant might have meant delay sufficient to thwart the purpose. In still others, it would appear that there was little or no concern by officers and agents to comply with even rudimentary requirements for carrying out a valid search and seizure. In all of them, however, detection and apprehension and the obtaining and use of evidence seized could have been accomplished by observing the rules. Even so, a doubt is cast upon the rules of justice when those who may deserve punishment for criminal acts are the ones who seek the protection of guarantees far more frequently than those innocently caught up in the web of the law. Perhaps it is because the former by far outnumber the latter.

The judicial pronouncements presented thus far have been primarily about claims of invasions of privacy by U.S. agents. The claims of violations were made via the protections guaranteed by the Fourth and Fifth Amendments. Anything obtained illegally was inadmissible in federal court. It was to be excluded. But the exclusionary rule until fairly recently did not apply to cases tried in state courts in the absence of a state exclusionary rule. One of the most interesting developments in the interpretations of the U.S. Constitution is the applicability of the guarantees of the Bill of Rights to the states via the Fourteenth Amendment.

The U.S. Supreme Court now holds that the protections

47. *Ibid.*, 14.

accorded the individual in the Fourth and Fifth Amendments are, indeed, incorporated into the Fourteenth Amendment. But the justices are not in full agreement about the manner of the incorporation or whether they were not there all along.

From 1833 until the adoption of the Fourteenth Amendment in 1868, claimed violations of the Bill of Rights by state and local governments found no comfort in the U.S. courts.[48] In 1886, in *Boyd, supra*, the protections of the Fourth and Fifth Amendments were interlocked and made interdependent. The Fourteenth Amendment "due process" did not, until recent years, provide these same guarantees against state and local governmental encroachments on the freedoms extended in the Bill of Rights as against the U.S. government. This had its beginnings about 1957. The development to "incorporate" the guarantees of the Bill of Rights into the Fourteenth Amendment has been rapid and is now considered virtually complete.[49]

In the *Mapp* case[50] of 1961 the full force of the Fourth Amendment was made applicable to all governments of the United States, and three years later in *Malloy*[51] the guarantees of the Fifth Amendment were imposed similarly.

These are striking developments, not because they came about, but because they came about so recently. In 1937, the only one of the Bill of Rights to be in full effect against state and local governmental encroachments was the First Amendment, with portions of the Fifth, Sixth, and the Seventh.[52] But by the end of 1968 the majority of the Court

48. *Barron* v. *Baltimore*, 7 Peters 243 (1833).

49. One of the best presentations on the incorporation development is Henry J. Abraham, *Freedom and the Court* (New York: Oxford Press, 1967), ch. 4, "The Fascinating World of 'Due Process of Law.'"

50. *Mapp* v. *U.S.*, 367 U.S. 643 (1961).

51. *Malloy* v. *Hogan*, 378 U.S. 1 (1964). The same day the Court handed down the decision in *Murphy* v. *Waterfront Commission*, 378 U.S. 52, 79, saying, "We hold that a state witness may not be compelled to give testimony which may be incriminating under federal law unless the compelled testimony and its fruits cannot be used in any manner by federal officials in connection with a criminal prosecution against him."

52. See Abraham, *Freedom and the Court*, p. 58.

considered the Bill of Rights mostly applicable to all governments—national, state, and local.

That there has not been unanimity among the members of the High Court is best expressed by the dissent from Justice Harlan in the 1964 *Malloy* case. He wrote cryptically that the "elaboration of *Mapp* in *Ker* v. *California* . . . did in my view make the Fourth Amendment applicable to the States through the Fourteenth; but there is nothing in it to suggest that the Fifth Amendment went along as baggage." [53]

It is not intended here to review the gradual incorporation in a case-by-case analysis. But the members of the Supreme Court have from time to time given expressions about the application of safeguards notwithstanding dual citizenship or different standards based upon concepts of the division of powers between the states and the national government. To Justice Cardozo, for example, the Fourteenth Amendment always incorporated the "superior" rights of the Bill of Rights. This was first expressed and applied to the First Amendment by Justice Sanford in the *Gitlow* case of 1925,[54] when he spoke of extending protection against state "abridgement."

> For the present purposes we may and do assume that freedom of speech and of the press—which are now protected by the First Amendment from abridgement by Congress—are among the fundamental personal rights and "liberties" protected by the due process clause of the Fourteenth Amendment from impairment by the states.

During the next three decades the protections of the Bill of Rights were being gradually extended. Justice Black has not agreed with the gradualism nor the notion of incorporation. He takes the position that the inclusion of the content of the Bill of Rights into the Fourteenth Amendment extends only to those guarantees specifically spelled out in the document, nothing more, nothing less. He has repeatedly said that there

53. *Malloy* v. *Hogan*, 378 U.S. 21. *Ker* v. *California*, 374 U.S. 23, involved a search and seizure of marijuana in plain view of arresting officer.

54. *Gitlow* v. *N.Y.*, 268 U.S. 652, 666.

is no reason for any step-by-step incorporation because the rights enumerated were already in the Fourteenth Amendment when it was adopted. The conclusion is the same, but the route is different.

Black especially parted company with the majority opinion in *Griswold, supra,* but his philosophy would not favor any agreement with the concurring opinion by Justice Goldberg, with the chief justice and Justice Brennan joining. "The framers of the Constitution believed that there are additional fundamental rights, protected from governmental infringement, which exist alongside those fundamental rights specifically mentioned in the first eight constitutional amendments." [55]

We do not know from the opinion what those additional rights are, but it suggests an interesting future development.

Although since *Mapp* in 1961 the state courts have not been free to permit illegally gained evidence to be introduced into a trial, the situation in those courts prior thereto is well expressed in the majority opinion in *Wolf* v. *Colorado*.

> The precise question for consideration is this: Does a conviction by a State Court for a State offense deny the "due process of law" required by the Fourteenth Amendment, solely because evidence that was admitted at the trial was obtained under circumstances which would have rendered it inadmissible in a prosecution for violation of a federal law in a court of the United States because there deemed to be an infraction of the Fourth Amendment . . .? The notion that the "due process of law" guaranteed by the Fourteenth Amendment is shorthand for the first eight amendments of the Constitution and thereby incorporates them has been rejected by this Court again and again, after impressive consideration. [56]

This was but twelve years before the Court did exactly the opposite. [57] Nonetheless, in the above cited case, Justice Frankfurter, giving the majority view, was concerned about the right to privacy and said:

55. 381 U.S. 479, 488. The Black view prevails in a *de facto* sense.
56. 338 U.S. 25, 26 (1949). Some states had an exclusionary rule.
57. *Mapp* v. *Ohio*, 367 U.S. 643, extended the exclusionary rule nationwide.

The security of one's privacy against arbitrary intrusion by the police—which is at the core of the Fourth Amendment—is basic to a free society. It is therefore implicit in "the concept of ordered liberty" and as such enforceable against the States through the Due Process Clause. . . . But the ways of enforcing such a basic right raise questions of a different order. How such arbitrary conduct should be checked, what remedies against it should be afforded, the means by which the right should be made effective, are all questions that are not to be so dogmatically answered as to preclude the varying solutions which spring from an allowable range of judgment on issues not susceptible of quantitative solution. . . . But the immediate question is whether the basic right to protection against arbitrary intrusion by the police demands the exclusion of logically relevant evidence obtained by an unreasonable search and seizure because, in a federal prosecution for a federal crime, it would be excluded.[58]

He then found support for his position by referring to the fact that most of the English-speaking world does not regard such protection as vital, and if the states wanted to include such ill-gotten evidence they should be free to do so.[59]

Illustrative of the development of the incorporation theory is the 1952 case of *Rochin* v. *California*.[60] It will be considered

58. 338 U.S. 25, 27, 28. Before *Weeks*, twenty-six states had opposed the doctrine; one anticipated it. After *Weeks* forty-seven states passed on the matter. Six observed it; fourteen rejected it. As of the date of *Wolf*, thirty states rejected it; seventeen agreed. *Weeks* v. *U.S.* 232 U.S. 383 (1914).

59. Frankfurter observed that of ten jurisdictions in the United Kingdom and the British Commonwealth of Nations, ten had passed on the rule, and none had held evidence obtained by illegal search and seizure inadmissible. The Lord Chief Justice said in 1955 that "the test to be applied in considering whether evidence is admissible is whether it is relevant to the matters at issue. If it is, it is admissible, and the court is not concerned with how the evidence was obtained." *Kuruma, Son of Kaniu* v. *The Queen*, A.C. 197, 203 (P.C.). Cited in David Fellman, *The Defendant's Rights Under English Law* (Madison: University of Wisconsin Press, 1966), p. 58.

60. 342 U.S. 165 (1952).

again in a later chapter, but is presented here to show the problem the Court had in protecting an invasion of privacy within the due process clause of the Fourteenth Amendment.

On the morning of July 1, 1949, three deputy sheriffs of the County of Los Angeles approached the home of Rochin, and finding the door open, entered, and then went to the second floor forcing open the door to his bedroom. They found him sitting partly dressed on the side of the bed. His wife was lying on the bed. The deputies saw two capsules on a small table beside the bed and asked, "Whose stuff is this?" Thereupon, Rochin picked up the capsules and put them in his mouth. The officers then attempted to extract them, but he had swallowed them.

He was then taken to a hospital and at the direction of one of the officers a doctor forced an emetic solution through a tube into Rochin's stomach—against his will—and produced vomiting, which in turn produced the capsules. Rochin was brought to trial on the charge of possessing a preparation of morphine in violation of the California Code. The chief evidence against him, of course, was the two capsules. The case later on reached the U.S. Supreme Court.

In his opinion for the Court, Justice Frankfurter noted that in the federal system the administration of justice "is predominately committed to the care of the States" and "broadly speaking, crimes in the United States are what the laws of the individual states make them . . . ." Accordingly,

> . . . we must be deeply mindful of the responsibilities of the States for the enforcement of criminal laws, and exercise with due humility our merely negative function in subjecting convictions from state courts to the very narrow scrutiny which the Due Process Clause . . . authorizes.[61]

But Frankfurter said that as the states have responsibilities, so also does the U.S. Supreme Court. A regard for the requirements of the Due Process Clause of the Fourteenth Amendment "inescapably imposes upon this Court an exercise of

61. *Ibid.*, 168, citing *Malinski* v. *N.Y.*, 324 U.S. 401 (1945).

judgment upon the whole court of proceedings . . . in order to ascertain whether they offend those canons of decency and fairness which express the notions of justice of English-speaking peoples toward those charged with the most heinous offenses."[62] Recognizing perhaps that the opinion would not be altogether popularly received in law enforcement quarters, he continued:

> Restraints on our jurisdiction are self-imposed only in the sense that there is from our decisions no immediate appeal short of impeachment or constitutional amendment. But that does not make due process of law a matter of judicial caprice. The faculties of the Due Process Clause may be indefinite and vague, but the mode of their ascertainment is not self-willed.[63]

The he got to the meat of the Court's objection to the methods by which Rochin had been delivered up of the capsules.

> This is conduct that shocks the conscience. Illegally breaking into the privacy of the petitioner, the struggle to open his mouth and remove what was there, the forcible extraction of his stomach's contents—the course of proceeding by agents of government to obtain evidence is bound to offend even hardened sensibilities. They are methods too close to the rack and screw to permit of constitutional differentiation.[64]

On the night of June 10, 1965, two police officers of the city of Lorain, Ohio, left their assigned cruising district and drove to 1420–1422 Broadway because they "suspected a crime was being committed there." They based their trip on tips from persons who stopped them on the street.

Upon arrival, the officers observed a number of cars parked in the immediate vicinity, and they observed the owner,

62. 342 U.S. 169.

63. *Ibid.*, 165, 172.

64. *Ibid.*, 172. Justice Black disagreed, saying: "But I believe that faithful adherence to the specific guarantees in the Bill of Rights insures a more permanent protection of individual liberty than that which can be afforded by the nebulous standards stated by the majority." *Ibid.*, 175.

Recznik, who was outside. They advised him there had better not be anything illegal going on inside. They told him they would return in half an hour.

Twenty minutes later the officers returned and saw that numerous cars were still parked in the area near the Recznik properties and saw several men enter the upstairs area. The officers then went upstairs, listened, and tried to look through a window and a door. Then they walked in unannounced. Recznik told them they couldn't come in. But one of the officers saw a dice game in progress, and they seized the table, chips, dice, and money and made arrests. They then continued to search the premises and, after finding some keys, proceeded to search the buildings; in a lower level they found some gambling paraphernalia which was also seized. Recznik was convicted and he appealed. The Court of Appeals confirmed his conviction.

The U.S. Supreme Court in considering the case said it could not agree that the "knowledge of the officers revealed by this record amounted to probable cause to believe that a crime was being committed." The Court noted that even the trial judge ordered a comment by one of the officers that the building was a "noted gambling joint" be stricken from the record. No effort, said the Court, was made to show that Recznik was connected with illicit gambling operations, nor did the prosecution even attempt to establish that the informers were reliable. "Even where a search is obtained, the police must show a basis for the search beyond the mere fact of an assertion by an informer. . . . At least as much is required to support a search without a warrant." [65]

A few additional cases involving search and seizure and claimed use of illegally obtained evidence still need mention. Prior to the application of the exclusionary rule to all courts, federal and state, there were practices of federal-state cooperation in obtaining evidence. State and local officers would obtain the evidence, often illegally, and hand it over to federal officials for use in a criminal trial.

65. *Recznik* v. *City of Lorain*, —— U.S. ——, decided November 18, 1968.

In *Lustig* v. *U.S.*,[66] a counterfeiting case, the charge was made that evidence obtained illegally by city police could not be used by federal officials at a federal trial.

One Sunday in March, 1946, a U.S. Secret Service agent received two telephone calls, one from the city police and one from the manager of a hotel. The reports indicated that violations of the counterfeiting statutes were being carried out in a room at the hotel. The agent went to the hotel, then to the room in question, and looked through the keyhole. There he saw a man, two brief cases, a large suitcase, but nothing to suggest any counterfeiting. Then the agent, Greene, talked to the chambermaid who apparently was the source of the original calls. Greene then left the hotel, went to the police station, and reported what he had seen, but also that he was certain "something was going on." Thereupon the local police obtained a warrant for arrest for violation of an ordinance requiring "known criminals" to register with the police. The police went to the hotel room, searched it in the absence of the registered guests, and found evidence of counterfeiting. Greene was not present during the search, but arrived later. He examined the evidence and was present shortly afterward when the defendants arrived at their hotel room.

The question was whether the evidence seized could be used against the persons arrested. The trial judge admitted the evidence because he did not see any "connivance or arrangement" on the part of Greene to have an illegal search made to get evidence he could not secure under federal law. The U.S. Supreme Court accepted that judicial pronouncement as fact. But the Court was not willing to let the events prevail and put a stamp of approval on the police action. Justice Frankfurter wrote:

> The uncontroverted facts show that before the search was concluded Greene was called in, and although he himself did not help empty the physical containers of the seized articles he did share in the critical examination of the uncovered articles as the physical search proceeded. It surely can make no difference whether a state officer

66. 338 U.S. 74 (1949).

turns up the evidence and hands it over to a federal
agent for his critical inspection with the view to its use
in a federal prosecution, or the federal agent himself
takes the articles out of a bag. It would trivialize law to
base legal significance on such a differentiation.[67]

The prosecution had relied on *Byars* v. *U.S.*[68] in claiming
no violation for the method by which the evidence was obtained. "The crux of that doctrine," wrote Frankfurter, "is
that a search is a search by a federal officer if he had a hand
in it; it is not a search by a federal officer if evidence secured
by state authorities is turned over to the federal authorities on
a silver platter."[69] But Frankfurter would not support the
doctrine in this case.

The evil of the matter to Frankfurter was participation by
a U.S. agent. "It is immaterial whether a federal agent
originated the idea or joined in it while the search is in progress.
So long as he was in it before the object of the search was
completely accomplished, he must be deemed to have participated in it."[70] Thus, the niceties of federal-state cooperation
were convenient, but not valid.

Shortly after the *Byars* decision, the Court had another
case involving federal-state cooperation. In *Gambino*,[71] decided
in 1927, New York authorities performed an unauthorized
search of an automobile, and the evidence was given to
federal authorities to assist in obtaining a conviction for
alleged bootlegging. At that time many states followed the
English rule and permitted illegally obtained evidence to be
admitted at a trial. But in this case, the U.S. Supreme Court
thought the extent of cooperation extreme and the method
by which the evidence was obtained was violative of the
accused's rights.

Automobiles and highway travel permit persons violating
criminal laws not only to commit crimes more easily and
quickly, but also to leave the scene with speed and arrive at

67. *Ibid.*, 78.   68. 273 U.S. 28 (1927).
69. *Lustig* v. *U.S.*, 78, 79.   70. *Ibid.*, 79.
71. *Gambino* v. *US.*, 275 U.S. 310.

distant points often before the criminal act is detected. The courts have been more willing to sanction the practice of stopping automobiles, searching them, and seizing evidence than would be supported in searching and seizing evidence in a residence or other premises, or even on the person. To require a search warrant or arrest warrant would likely mean the fleeing automobile would long be gone to a distant point and any evidence disposed of. But two cases illustrate problems of carrying out a presumption of wrongdoing and the broader practice of arrests and searches without warrants.

In 1961, William Beck was driving his automobile in the vicinity of East 115th Street in Cleveland, Ohio. He was accosted by the Cleveland police who ordered him to pull to the curb. The police had no arrest or search warrant. But they placed Beck under arrest and searched his car. They found nothing of interest. Nonetheless, they took him to a nearby police station where they searched his person. They found an envelope containing a number of "clearing house slips" beneath the sock of his leg. He was thereupon charged with violating the "numbers racket" laws. At the trial he sought to have the slips suppressed as evidence, but he was unsuccessful. His conviction was appealed to the higher courts of Ohio, both affirming his conviction.

The U.S. Supreme Court took the case and decided against the use of the evidence.[72] The opinion indicated concern whether the police had any solid grounds for stopping Beck, arresting him, searching his car, or taking him to the police station and then searching him. It questioned whether

> the moment the arrest was made, the officers had probable cause to make it—whether at that moment the facts and circumstances within their knowledge and of which they had reasonably trustworthy information were sufficient to warrant a prudent man in believing the petitioner had committed or was committing an offense.[73]

The opinion noted that the officer who made the arrest stated at the trial that he had reports about Beck and that he

72. *Beck* v. *Ohio*, 379 U.S. 89 (1964).
73. *Ibid.*, 91.

was involved in the numbers racket. He further stated that he planned to stop Beck if he came into his patrol area of the city. But the U.S. Court found this insufficient cause. "And the record does not show that the officers saw the petitioner 'stop' before they arrested him, . . . or otherwise perceived anything else to give them ground for belief that the petitioner had acted or was acting unlawfully."[74] The State of Ohio claimed that the police had acted in good faith and had found evidence of their suspicions. But this did not help much.

> We may assume that the officers acted in good faith in arresting the petitioner. But "good faith" on the part of the arresting officers is not enough . . . . If subjective good faith alone were the test, the protections of the Fourth Amendment would evaporate, and the people would be "secure in their persons, houses, papers, and effects," only in the discretion of the police.[75]

Another car search is pertinent. The FBI had observed persons loading some boxes into a car in an alley in a residential district. They had been advised earlier that some contraband whisky was being hunted, and the activities in the alley caused the agents to be suspicious. They followed the car, stopped it, caused a search to be made, all without any warrant, and found contraband—not whisky, but stolen radios. In *Henry* v. *U.S.*,[76] the U.S. Supreme Court said that there had to be probable cause before the car was stopped and the arresting officers got it by looking through the car door or window. It said that common rumor or reports of suspicion or even a strong reason to suspect was not adequate to support even a warrant for arrest. "It is true," went the opinion, "that a federal crime had been committed at a terminal in the neighborhood." That one in the auto had a record of association with stolen equipment was not enough, for the rumor about him was "practically meaningless."[77] To the Court, the act of riding in a car, stopping in an alley, and picking up packages are innocent acts. If the acts had been at or near a trucking terminal or interstate truck, it

74. *Ibid.*, 94.   75. *Ibid.*, 97.
76. 361 U.S. 98 (1959).   77. *Ibid.*, 103.

might have been justified, but the fact that the radios were stolen did not mean that every man who carries a package is subject to arrest or the package subject to seizure.

It is not unusual in police searches to uncover evidence of law violations not anticipated. Illustrative is *Mapp* v. *Ohio*.[78] Miss Mapp was convicted by an Ohio court of knowingly having had in her possession and under her control certain lewd and lascivious books, pictures, and photographs in violation of the Ohio Code. But the police went to her home following a tip that a person was hiding in the home who was wanted in connection with a recent bombing.

Upon arriving at the Mapp house, the police knocked on the door and demanded entrance, but Miss Mapp refused. About three hours later the officers again sought entrance. When no one responded the police went to another door, forcibly opened it, and gained entrance. Meanwhile, Miss Mapp's attorney arrived, but the police would not permit him to see her or to enter the house.

> It appears that Miss Mapp was halfway down the stairs from the upper floor to the front door when the officers, in this highhanded manner, broke into the hall. She demanded to see the search warrant. A paper, claimed to be a warrant was held up by one of the officers. She grabbed the "warrant" and placed it in her bosom. A struggle ensued in which the officers recovered the piece of paper.[79]

She was handcuffed and forcibly taken upstairs to her bedroom, where the officers searched the room. Next, the search spread through the rest of the second floor, and then to the basement. The obscene materials were found in the course of the search. In the trial no search warrant was produced by the prosecution, nor was the failure to produce one explained or accounted for. In his opinion for the U.S. Supreme Court, Justice Clark wrote:

> Today we once again examine . . . the right to privacy free from unreasonable state intrusion, and . . . are led . . .

78. 367 U.S. 643 (1961).
79. *Ibid.*, 644.

to close the only courtroom door remaining open to evidence secured by official lawlessness in flagrant abuse of that basic right, reserved to all persons as a specific guarantee against that very same unlawful conduct. We hold that all evidence obtained by searches and seizures in violation of the Constitution is, . . . inadmissible in a state court.

　　Since the Fourth Amendment's right of privacy has been declared enforceable against the States through the Due Process Clause of the Fourteenth, it is enforceable against them by the same sanction of exclusion as is used against the Federal Government.[80]

Clark believed that holding the exclusionary rule to be a part of both the Fourth and Fourteenth Amendments was not only a logical "dictate of prior cases, but it also makes very good sense."[81] Double standards were no longer acceptable.

If it was good sense, it was not long before the question would be raised as to how far the rule would be applied. One of the first of these was *Ker* v. *California*.[82] It involved a conviction for possession of marijuana in violation of the California Code. At the trial the petitioners, husband and wife, contended that their arrests were improper because the evidence was taken after a search and without a warrant or probable cause. It seemed that a police officer observed through an open door what appeared to him to be a package of marijuana on the kitchen sink. He entered and proceeded to search and arrest. More marijuana was found in the bedroom.

The opinion was written by Justice Clark who also wrote the majority opinion in *Mapp*. In *Ker* he endeavored to spell out what was and what was not decided in *Mapp*. He said that the *Mapp* case established no assumption of supervisory authority over the state courts, and implied no total obliteration of state laws relating to arrests and search in favor of federal law. "Mapp sounded no death knell for federalism; rather . . ." that "a healthy federalism depends upon the

80. *Ibid.*, 654, 655.
81. *Ibid.*, 657.
82. 374 U.S. 23 (1963).

avoidance of needless conflict between state and federal courts . . . ."[83] He insisted that *Mapp* did not attempt the "impossible task of laying down a 'fixed formula' for the application in specific cases of the constitutional prohibition against unreasonable searches and seizures; . . ." but rather recognized that the Court would be met with recurring questions about what was reasonable. Then he reaffirmed the view about reasonableness in the *Mapp* search. "The search involved there was clearly unreasonable and bore no stamp of legality . . . ."[84]

Clark restated the general rules applicable to reasonableness in making an arrest under the conditions found in the investigation of the Ker home. He concluded that the facts supported the entry and that the arrest was legal. But what of the search? The evidence was in plain view, and it did not matter whether there was time or whether it was practical to have gone for a search warrant. "The doctrine that a search without a warrant may be lawfully conducted if incident to a lawful arrest has long been recognized as consistent with the Fourth Amendment's protection against unreasonable searches and seizures."[85]

The aftermath of *Mapp* was one of widespread criticism by law enforcement officers, judges, and others who believed that the exclusionary rule for state cases would make law enforcement extremely difficult. One such view was expressed a few years afterward by then Commissioner of New York City Police, Michael J. Murphy.[86] He reported that it was necessary for the police department to revise their instructions to the police and to retrain them in arrest and search and seizure procedures. He thought that the time so spent would have been better used on regular duty. But he said his department did make an effort to comply even if it plagued law enforce-

83. *Ibid.*, 31, citing *Elkins* v. *U.S.*, 364 U.S. 206 (1960).
84. 374 U.S., 31.
85. *Ibid.*, 41.
86. "Judicial Review of Police Methods in Law Enforcement—The Problems of Compliance by Police Departments," *Texas Law Review* 44, no. 5 (April 1966): 939–946.

ment "in its practical implementation." In the four and one half years following *Mapp*, he reported his department had obtained some 17,889 search warrants, but he complained that it was not easy to have stenographers handy at all hours of the night nor on holidays, nor to find the magistrate to obtain his approval.

Aside from these concerns, Murphy's chief question was the difficulty in defining what constitutes a lawful arrest and the search and seizure which might follow. It bothered him particularly that the courts had not been able to help them much in formulating rules which were appropriate for the "practical application on the firing line."

It was anticipated that there would be an early test whether the decision in *Mapp* would be retroactive. But the U.S. Supreme Court made short work of that issue in *Linkletter* v. *Walker*, decided in 1965.

> The misconduct of the police prior to *Mapp* has already occurred and will not be corrected by releasing the prisoners involved. Nor would it add harmony to the delicate state-federal relationship of which we have spoken. . . . Finally, the ruptured privacy of the victims' homes and effects cannot be restored. Reparation comes too late.[87]

Law enforcement officers have broad authority to make arrests as a result of illegal actions committed in their presence or view. It is another matter if the arrest comes after a search without observing the limitations of probable cause. The policeman has a right to search a person being lawfully arrested, however, if he seeks dangerous weapons, or to prevent the destruction of evidence. These conditions were involved in the 1968 "stop and frisk" cases. One of these was *Terry* v. *Ohio*.[88]

87. 381 U.S. 618, 637. In *Fuller* v. *Alaska*, ——— U.S. ———, decided October 28, 1968, the U.S. Supreme Court held that a telegram allegedly sent by Fuller and introduced as evidence by the prosecution in a criminal case involving shooting with intent to kill or wound, claimed to violate section 605 of the FCC Act, not enough to reverse the conviction even though it violated the decision in *Lee*.

88. 392 U.S. 1, decided June 10, 1968.

John W. Terry was convicted of carrying a concealed weapon and was sentenced. Evidence at the trial included two revolvers and bullets seized from him and a codefendant. The arresting officer testified he saw them standing on a street corner, that he had never seen them before, but that he had developed routine habits during nearly forty years as a policeman in watching people as they walked about the streets. He stated that in observing the two men, "when I looked over they did not look right to me." As they walked along shop windows and retraced their route, then walked off again together, he became suspicious and thought it looked like "casing a job." He considered it his duty to investigate. He feared, he said, they "may have a gun."

He stopped Terry and his companion and questioned them. He then searched Terry and found a gun but was unable to remove it. He directed them to go inside a nearby store. Then he removed Terry's overcoat, retrieved a .38 caliber revolver, and ordered the men to face the wall with hands raised. "So far as it appears from the record," went the U.S. Supreme Court opinion, "the officer never put his hands beneath the outer garments." A motion was made to suppress the introduction of the revolver and the bullets at the trial, but without success.

After reviewing the kinds of street encounters which take place between citizen and the police, from friendly exchanges to hostile confrontations of armed men, the U.S. Supreme Court turned attention to the question whether it is always unreasonable for a policeman to seize a person and subject him to a limited search for weapons unless there is a probable cause for arrest.

It must be recognized that whenever a police officer accosts an individual and restrains his freedom, his freedom to walk away, he has "seized" that person. And it is nothing less than sheer torture of the English language to suggest that a careful exploration of the outer surfaces of a person's clothing all over his or her body in an attempt to find weapons is not a "search." Moreover, it is simply fantastic to urge that such a procedure performed in public by a policeman while the citizen stands helpless, perhaps facing a wall with his hands raised, is a "petty indignity." It is a serious intrusion upon the sanctity of the person, which may inflict great indignity and arouse strong resentment, and is not to be taken lightly.[89]

The decision was not to turn on the propriety of Officer McFadden's investigation of Terry's behavior, but whether "there was justification for McFadden's invasion of Terry's personal security by searching him for weapons in the course of that investigation."

> We are now concerned with more than the governmental interest in investigating crimes; in addition, there is a more immediate interest of the police officer in taking steps to assure himself that the person with whom he is dealing is not armed with a weapon that could unexpectedly and fatally be used against him. Certainly it would be unreasonable to require that police officers take unneccessary risks in the performance of their duties. American criminals have a long tradition of armed violence, and every year in this country many law enforcement officers are killed in the line of duty, and thousands more are wounded. Virtually all of these deaths and a substantial portion of the injuries are inflicted with guns and knives.
>
> In view of these facts we cannot blind ourselves to the need for law enforcement officers to protect themselves and other prospective victims of violence in situations where they may lack probable cause for arrest.[90]

Was there probable cause for what McFadden did? Was the search justified since the search constituted "a severe, although brief intrusion upon cherished personal security, and it must surely be an annoying, frightening, and perhaps humiliating experience."

The chief justice apparently wanted those who read his words to be certain that he was mindful of the rights to privacy, but also to give recognition to what McFadden claimed "a reasonably prudent man" would have been warranted in doing, that is, believing that Terry was armed. It was a matter of self-preservation on the policeman's part.

89. *Ibid.*, 16, 17.
90. *Ibid.*, 23, 24.

"The sole justification of the search . . . is the protection of the police officer and others nearby, and it must therefore be confined in scope to an intrusion reasonably designed to discover guns, knives, clubs, or other hidden instruments for the assault of the police officer."[91] Thus, McFadden's search was proper and within bounds.

On the other hand, all "suspicious" characters coming within the view of the police patrolman may not be so properly and validly searched. The companion case to *Terry* was *Sibron* v. *N.Y.*[92]

Nelson Sibron was convicted for the unlawful possession of heroin. From the record it appears that police officer Martin observed Sibron for several hours prior to midnight and, among other actions, saw that he talked with several people Martin said were known narcotic addicts. He did not hear any of the conversations and saw nothing else that would be called suspicious. Later, Sibron entered a restaurant and from the outside Martin saw him talk with more known addicts. Martin heard nothing that was said and saw nothing pass between Sibron and any of the men with whom he had talked. Sibron ordered pie and coffee and as he was eating, Martin approached him and asked him to come outside. Sibron complied, and once there Martin said, "You know what I'm after." The record is not clear what happened at that point, but hands were in and out of Sibron's pockets and some "glassine envelopes" containing heroin were discovered. In any event there was a request to suppress the use of the heroin as evidence. It was denied.

The U.S. Supreme Court opinion recognized that New York was free to develop its own law of search and seizure to meet the needs of law enforcement. It was also free to set standards by "any means it may choose." But, "it may not, however, authorize police conduct which trenches upon Fourth Amendment rights, regardless of the labels which it attaches to such conduct."[93] It did not matter whether the

91. *Ibid.*, 29.
92. 392 U.S. 40 (1968).
93. *Ibid.*, 61.

search had been authorized by state law. The question was whether the search was reasonable.

> . . . it is clear that the heroin was inadmissible. . . . The officer was not acquainted with Sibron and had no information concerning him. He merely saw Sibron talking to a number of . . . addicts. . . . [He] was completely ignorant of the content of these conversations, . . . saw nothing pass between Sibron and the addicts. So far as he knew, they might indeed "have been talking about the World Series."[94]

The Court considered it unreasonable to infer that persons who talk with narcotic addicts are engaged in the criminal traffic. Officer Martin lacked probable cause. But if he lacked probable cause, "his seizure . . . might still have been justified at the outset if he had reasonable ground to believe Sibron was armed and dangerous." To the Court, Officer Martin's testimony revealed no such facts.[95]

On April 7, 1969, the U.S. Supreme Court ruled on a privacy situation which may have far-reaching implications.[96] Labeled an "obscenity" case, the Court in an opinion without dissent declared in strong language that even if obscene materials are found in a home, the right to have it is protected by the U.S. Constitution.

Justice Marshall said that "if the First Amendment means anything, it means that a State has no business telling a man, sitting alone in his own house, what books he may read or what films he may watch." He considered that the entire heritage of Constitutional rights "rebels at the thought of giving government the power to control men's minds."[97] This decision apparently is the first one by the U.S. Supreme Court determining whether mere possession of what is described by law as obscene matter can be a crime. The Court was emphatic in saying no. The First Amendment protects a man's right "to satisfy his intellectual and emotional needs

94. *Ibid.*, 62.
95. *Ibid.*, 64.
96. *Stanley* v. *Georgia*, ——— U.S. ———.
97. *Ibid.*

in the privacy of his own home," even if it includes satisfying them with obscene movies.

In this case, federal and state officers raided bachelor Robert Eli Stanley's home in Atlanta, Georgia, on suspicion of conducting illegal gambling. They did not find any evidence of gambling, but during the search they found three rolls of .8-millimeter film in a desk drawer, and with Stanley's viewer saw what they contained. They reported them to be a succession of "orgies by nude men and women engaging in repeated acts of seduction, sodomy and sexual intercourse."[98] Stanley was convicted of possessing obscene material violative of a Georgia statute. In overturning the conviction, the Court restricted its ruling to the First Amendment guarantees protecting freedom of speech and press. It did not open the door to "orgies" which might actually take place in a home, but it is not idle to speculate that a case of that sort may well reach the Court one day in anticipation of greater freedom in home activities.

The right to privacy reflected in these cases mostly involved those caught in law violations. This is as might be expected since law may restrict human conduct and human beings object to these man-made restraints. Society has determined that some actions are unacceptable and has made them subject to punishment. Those carrying out these mandates, however, frequently go beyond the law of the land and, when done and contested, have had their actions reversed.

It is natural that the police will seek all means available to them to ferret out those who break the law. They will use every technique known to them. It is their responsibility to bring to justice those who harm the liberties, person, and property of others. In the cases here presented, the central theme has been upon the constitutional requirement that

98. *New York Times*, April 8, 1969, pp. 1, 18. Justices Stewart, White, and Brennan indicated they thought the Court opinion should have disapproved also the method by which the films were obtained, since the warrant covered only the possibility of finding gambling apparatus.

privacy be respected within reasonable limits. Most enforcement officers, some judges, and others interested consider the judicial pronouncements of reasonable restraint as stacking the rules in favor of the criminal suspect. There are no complete data to prove that police are generally thwarted in their jobs as a result, nor that evidence gained illegally and therefore not admissible in a trial in fact has meant that any substantial number of offenders are on the loose. The census of jails and penitentiaries give clues to the contrary.

This chapter has not presented the law of arrest or of search and seizure. It has, rather, indicated the trend of judicial pronouncement, primarily by the U.S. Supreme Court, about the right to privacy as arrest and search and seizure relate to that right. Generally speaking, a search is unreasonable without a warrant. But there are exceptions. If there is reason to believe that contraband is in an automobile or boat, to wait to obtain a warrant could mean that the automobile or boat would soon be gone and beyond the reach of the jurisdiction of the warrant. Thus, a search might be proper if there was probable cause. In the "stop and frisk" cases of 1968, a search was proper if done to discover weapons. And a search incident to arrest, if proper, must be done at the place of the arrest and not at another place not covered by the warrant. On the other hand, a search which was legal but did not turn up the evidence sought but which disclosed other evidence of crime was legal if possession was a crime.

A search is proper without a warrant if there is probable cause and more than mere suspicion. Even the word of a paid informer on an affidavit is sufficient, and his name need not be disclosed. But in any event, there must be some observation that all of these actions bear the label of essential fairness in their execution.

III

Rights in Conflict

———◆———

"To say that the 'constitution guaranteed' one class of rights more than the other would be to an Englishman an unnatural or senseless form of speech." So wrote Dicey in his *Law of the Constitution.*[1]

Not so in the United States. At least not so if we accept the judicial pronouncements that some rights have a preferred or superior position and must be recognized as such. If some rights have a superior position over others, then when they are in conflict the inferior one must give way to the superior right. In this chapter consideration will be given to some U.S. Supreme Court decisions and opinions in which the superior rights come into conflict with other rights and with the right to privacy. The subsequent chapter will consider the right to privacy and its conflict with the exercise of the police power of the states.

In his 1937 opinion in *Palko* v. *Connecticut,*[2] Justice Cardozo indicated a double standard in basic human rights. He sought to distinguish between the rights he considered as "of the very essence of a scheme of ordered liberty" and those rights which were important but without which "justice would not perish." These latter rights were important but were not "implicit in the concept of ordered liberty." He believed that

1. A. V. Dicey, *Introduction to the Study of the Law of the Constitution,* 8th ed. (London: Macmillan & Co., 1920), pp. 196, 197.
2. 302 U.S. 319 (1937).

there were rights having a higher status and were "those fundamental principles of liberty and justice" which are at the base of all our civil and political institutions.

He wrote that the right to trial by jury and a guarantee of immunity from prosecution except through the indictment procedure "may have value and importance," but they are not of the very essence of "a scheme of ordered liberty." If they were abolished it would not "violate a 'principle of justice so rooted in the traditions and conscience of our people as to be ranked as fundamental.' "[3] And he continued, saying that

> few would be so narrow or provincial as to maintain that a fair and enlightened system of justice would be impossible without them. What is true of jury trials and indictments is true also, as the cases show, of the immunity from compulsory self-incrimination. . . . This too might be lost, and justice still be done.[4]

To Cardozo, those immunities which are valid "as against the federal government," which have been found by "force of the specific pledges of particular amendments to be implicit in the concept of ordered liberty" through the Fourteenth Amendment, "become valid against the states." In speaking of the absorption of fundamental rights into the Fourteenth Amendment, he wrote:

> If the Fourteenth Amendment has absorbed them, the process of absorption has had its source in the belief that neither liberty nor justice would exist if they were sacrificed . . . . This is true, for illustration, of freedom of thought, and speech. Of that freedom one may say that it is the matrix, the indispensable condition, of nearly every other form of freedom.[5]

Twenty years later, in his dissenting opinion in *Roth* v. *U.S.*,[6] Justice Douglas wrote of the preferred position of some

3. *Ibid.*, 325. Citing *Snyder* v. *Massachusetts*, 291 U.S. 97, 105 (1934).
4. 302 U.S. 325.
5. *Ibid.*, 326, 327.
6. 354 U.S. 476 (1957).

rights. "The First Amendment, its prohibition in terms absolute, was designed to preclude courts as well as legislatures from weighing the values of speech against silence. The First Amendment puts free speech in a preferred position." [7]

The First Amendment is the only one which specifically uses the word "Congress" and forbids it from actions which would interfere with the freedoms or restraints listed. The other amendments of the Bill of Rights do not use the word "Congress," but it has been readily concluded that it was the source of restraint for all of the amendments. The First Amendment provides:

> Congress shall make no law respecting an establishment of religion, or prohibiting the free exercise thereof; or abridging the freedom of speech, or of the press; or the right of the people peaceably to assemble, and to petition the Government for a redress of grievances.

Since the words "freedom of speech" come after reference to the word "religion," it must be assumed that freedom of religion also has a preferred position. The free exercise of religion has been at issue frequently in the courts. Its exercise has come squarely into conflict with the right to privacy. It has come also into conflict with the exercise of the police power of the states.

Nearly thirty years ago in *Cantwell* v. *Connecticut*,[8] Justice Roberts, speaking for a majority of the U.S. Supreme Court, said that a state statute making it a crime for any person to solicit or canvass from house to house for any religious cause without prior approval of a public official constituted a "censorship of religion as a means of determining its right to survive" and would deny those so engaged the protections guaranteed by the Fourteenth Amendment. (The First and Fourteenth Amendments were then absorbed.) The amendment, wrote Roberts, thus "embraces two concepts—freedom to believe and freedom to act." Those engaged in the canvass for their religious cause were not found to have violated or

7. *Ibid.*, 514.
8. 310 U.S. 296 (1940).

invaded any right "or interest of the public or of the man accosted."⁹

Thus, the superior right of the free exercise of religion should prevail even though it might invade the privacy of those canvassed. There appears to be little doubt that the right, broadly construed, to the free exercise of religion is a right superior to any claimed right of privacy. Justice Black put the question about privacy in these words in his dissent in the *Griswold* case. "I like my privacy as well as the next one, but I am nevertheless compelled to admit that government has the right to invade it unless prohibited by some specific constitutional provisions."¹⁰ In *Cantwell* it was not government which invaded privacy, it was a private person. But government had tried to protect privacy and the "free exercise" of religion prevailed.

Some details about the *Cantwell* case are pertinent. The Cantwells were arrested because they were going from house to house in New Haven, Connecticut, asking the person who responded to their call for permission to play one or more phonograph records, which in turn explained some books and pamphlets on religious subjects. A Connecticut statute attempted to restrain such activities by requiring that anyone wishing to solicit for a religious cause would first have to obtain a permit or certificate from the state secretary of welfare indicating that the cause was a religious one. The statute was intended to prevent the very activities undertaken by the Cantwells.

In their solicitations, if a householder granted permission, a record or records would be played and an effort made to sell the books or pamphlets. If refused, then a request was made for a contribution. The religious cause was the Jehovah's Witnesses, and the Cantwells claimed to be ordained ministers of the Witnesses. The problem was that they chose a predominately Catholic neighborhood to do their soliciting, and Catholics do not like the attacks made on their religion by the Witnesses.

9. *Ibid.*, 303, 309.
10. 381 U.S. 479, 510 (1965).

The privacy of the householder was invaded by the ringing of the doorbell or a knock on the door. The question before the U.S. Supreme Court was whether the right to the free exercise of religion was supreme over the householder's right to freedom from interference not of his own choosing. Justice Roberts wrote the opinion and fully supported the free exercise of religion.

> We hold that the statute, as construed and applied to the appellants, deprives them of their liberty without due process of law. . . . The Fourteenth Amendment has rendered the legislatures of the states as incompetent as Congress to enact such laws. The constitutional inhibition of legislation on the subject of religion has a double aspect. On the one hand, it forestalls compulsion by law of the acceptance of any creed or the practice of any form of worship. Freedom of conscience and religion to adhere to such religious organization or form of worship as the individual may choose cannot be restricted by law. On the other hand, however, it safeguards the free exercise of the chosen form of religion . . . . Equally obvious is it that a state may not unduly suppress free communication of views, religious or other, under the guise of conserving desirable conditions.[11]

The Connecticut statute provided a method of prior restraint, and there were no appropriate standards to guide the state official in making his decision to grant or deny a certificate to a religious group. But Justice Roberts left the door ajar for future conflict which might arise between religious freedom and other freedoms including privacy. He wrote:

> Conviction . . . was not pursuant to a statute evincing a legislative judgment that street discussion of religious affairs, because of its tendency to provoke disorder, should be regulated, or a judgment that the playing of the phonograph on the streets should in the interests of comfort or privacy be limited or prevented.[12]

Three years later the opportunity came for the Court to recognize a right to privacy, but in the name of a superior

11. *Ibid.*, 303, 308.
12. *Ibid.*, 307.

position for the free exercise of religion, privacy lost. The Court held invalid a Struthers, Ohio, ordinance[13] which prohibited knocking on a householder's door or ringing his doorbell to deliver a handbill without his invitation. There was no requirement for a license or a permit. It was a prohibition against the ringing or the knocking without prior invitation to do so. The Court held the ordinance to be an unconstitutional abridgment of the religious freedom of the Jehovah's Witnesses.

The majority opinion suggested that if the householder wanted to avoid such visits all he had to do was to place a sign on the premises advising against such intrusions. Thus, even though the city had enacted an ordinance at the request of its citizens as a means of preventing unwanted intrusions, such an ordinance had to fall because practitioners of one religion who exercise it outside as well as inside a religious house cannot be restrained from carrying on in the streets and up to the doorstep.

Justice Black has strong views about the absolute position of supremacy of the specifics of the Bill of Rights.[14] When he reads the First Amendment he finds that there shall be "no law" respecting the free exercise of religion and to him "no" means that there will not be one. In the *Struthers* case the ordinance did not restrict its force to religious activity. It was a total prohibition on all types of unwanted solicitations. The decision turned on its adverse effect on freedom of speech and press even though it involved religious pamphlets. Justice Black wrote the opinion for the Court.

> The right of freedom of speech and press have broad scope. The authors of the First Amendment knew that novel and unconventional ideas might disturb the complacent, but they chose to encourage a freedom which they believed essential if vigorous enlightenment was even to triumph over slothful ignorance. This freedom

13. *Martin* v. *Struthers*, 319 U.S. 141 (1943).
14. See his dissent in *Adamson* v. *California*, 322 U.S. 71–72 (1947), and his views in *Everson* v. *Board of Education of Ewing Township*, 330 U.S. 1, 18 (1947).

embraces the right to distribute literature and the right to receive it. The privilege may not be withdrawn even if it creates the minor nuisance for a community of cleaning litter from its streets. . . . The ordinance does not control anything but the distribution of literature, and in that respect it substitutes the judgment of the community for the judgment of the householder.[15]

Ordinances of that sort were not unique. Many cities had enacted similar ordinances after the 1930's and are generally known by the title "Green River Ordinance" after the 1931 ordinance by Green River, Wyoming. Black wrote about them and their purposes in his opinion.

Ordinances of this sort now before us may be aimed at the protection of the householders from annoyance, including intrusion upon the hours of rest, and at the prevention of crime. Constant callers, whether selling pots or distributing leaflets, may lessen the peaceful enjoyment of a home as much as a neighborhood glue factory or railroad yard which zoning ordinances may prohibit.[16]

It was claimed of the Struthers ordinance that Struthers was an industrial city and many people had "swing shift" hours and worked nights, sleeping during the day, and the bell pushers interfered with the hours of sleep, "although they call at high noon." Even so, the right to distribute was supreme. "Freedom to distribute information . . . is so clearly vital to the preservation of a free society that, putting aside reasonable police and health regulations of time and manner of distribution, it must be fully preserved."[17]

Justice Reed dissented and supported the cause of privacy. He found nothing in the First Amendment which compelled anyone to listen to arguments on religion or politics.

Once the door is opened, the visitor may not insert his foot and insist upon a hearing. He certainly may not enter the home. To knock or ring, however, comes close to

15. *Martin* v. *Struthers*, 143, 144.
16. *Ibid.*, 144.
17. *Ibid.*, 146, 147.

such invasions. To prohibit such a call leaves open distribution of the notice on the street or at homes without signal to announce his deposit. Such assurance of privacy falls far short of an abridgement of freedom of the press. The ordinance seems a fair adjustment of the privileges of distributors and the rights of householders.[18]

Three years after *Struthers*, the Supreme Court was faced with another issue over religious freedom, again involving the Jehovah's Witnesses. This was a Texas case[19] involving a state statute making it an offense for a peddler or a hawkster of merchandise to refuse to leave permises after notice to leave. It is of interest because the statute was enforced in a village owned by the United States under a program of providing housing for persons engaged in national defense work. According to all indications, the village looked much like any other. It was open to the public and had the characteristics of a typical American town. The manager of the town had ordered the defendant, Tucker, to discontinue his religious activities in the town or to leave. He refused, was arrested, tried, and convicted.

The U.S. Supreme Court found nothing in the U.S. statutes or regulations which were intended to bar freedom of press and religion within villages such as the one in question. It was not, therefore, within the power of the manager, an employee of the government, to issue and enforce such rules. It was an unconstitutional abridgment of freedom of press and religion.

That same year a related case was heard, again involving the religious activities of a Jehovah's Witness.[20] This was an Alabama case and a statute making it a crime to enter or remain on the premises of another after being warned not to do so. It is similar to the prior case in Texas except that it involved a company-owned, and therefore a private, town. The town of Chickasaw was owned and operated by the Gulf Shipbuilding Corporation. Except for the fact that it was

18. *Ibid.*, 157.
19. *Tucker* v. *Texas*, 326 U.S. 517 (1946).
20. *Marsh* v. *Alabama*, 326 U.S. 501 (1946).

fully owned by the corporation, it had all the appearances of any other American town.

Grace Marsh, a Jehovah's Witness, came onto the town sidewalk, stood near the post office, and undertook to distribute religious literature. The corporation had posted notices in various places indicating that the town was private property and that without written permission soliciting was not permitted. Grace Marsh was warned that distribution was prohibited and that no permit to distribute would be forthcoming. She was asked to leave, then charged with violation of the statute. The Supreme Court opinion went thus:

> Our question then narrows down to this: Can those people who live in or come to Chickasaw be denied freedom of press and religion simply because a single company has legal title to all the town? We do not agree that the corporation's property interests settle the question. . . . Many people . . . live in company owned towns. These people, just as residents of municipalities, are free citizens. . . . To act as good citizens they must be informed. In order to enable them to be properly informed their information must be uncensored. There is no more reason for depriving these people of the liberties guaranteed by the First and Fourteenth Amendments than there is for curtailing these freedoms with respect to any other citizen.[21]

These decisions show that any claimed right to privacy has been put aside by the superior position of freedom of religion and of the press. If one wishes to prevent annoyances of the kind described he cannot expect his community to do it for him.

Or can he? It may depend upon where he lives. If he lives in a privately owned town, the town cannot prevent the intrusion. Neither can the public municipality do so. But can he achieve a degree of privacy from the door knockers and bell ringers in an apartment dwelling? The answer came in 1948 in still another case involving the Jehovah's Witnesses.

In *Watchtower Bible and Tract Society* v. *Metropolitan Life Insurance Company*,[22] the New York Court of Appeals found

21. *Ibid.*, 505, 508, 509.
22. 297 N.Y. 339 (1948).

that the Witnesses had gone too far in their claim for the free exercise of their First Amendment rights. The insurance company was the owner of a residential community in the Bronx known as Parkchester. It was said to be the largest development of its kind and housed more than 35,000 people in 171 adjoining and interrelated buildings. The buildings were from seven to twelve stories high. Through the development were two public highways and a number of private streets, lanes, and parks. All of the apartments were held under written lease.

The company's management had written regulations providing that no person or group of persons should enter any apartment building for the purposes of

> canvassing or of vending, peddling, or soliciting orders for any merchandise, device, book, periodical, pamphlet, circular, or for any printed, mimeographed, multigraphed or typewritten matter whatsoever; nor for the purpose of soliciting alms, religious, charitable or public institution or organization whatsoever. . . .

It also prohibited distribution of handbills and similar printed materials. Phonograph records could not be played in connection with any canvassing or distribution. But any of these restrictions could be waived upon the application and consent of the manager and the consent or invitation of the tenant.

In 1941 and into 1944 the society's members made visits into the area. They began by handing out leaflets on the streets, public and private, and going from door to door trying to interest residents or passersby. Some of the tenants accepted; some instructed company guards to prevent them. Several hundred Witnesses came after the suit was started and insisted on going into the interior passageways to every apartment requesting that the tenant certify that he did not object to the visit. Some eight thousand responded, but many testified "as to the persistency and the demands and the inconvenience suffered." The defendant urged that the society's members had a constitutional right to enter the apartment areas whether the occupants wanted them or not.

To the New York appellate court these activities were beyond the protections accorded by the First and Fourteenth Amendments. It was one thing to deny access to the streets and exterior ways of the development, but quite another to insist that there was a guaranteed right to intrude into "a narrow inner hallway on an upper floor of an apartment house. . . ." Such a place "is hardly an appropriate place at which to demand the free exercise of those ancient rights." [23]

It is most unfortunate that the generous guarantee of religious freedom and one so strongly supported by the courts should be in such continuous contest by one religious group.

In 1948 a case involving a Lockport, New York, ordinance reached the U.S. Supreme Court.[24] Samuel Saia had violated a sound-amplification ordinance which forbad the use of such devices unless done with the permission of the Chief of Police. Saia was refused a permit on the grounds that people had complained about his prior broadcasts of some talks on religious subjects. He proceeded anyway using loud-speakers in a small city-owned recreation park.

In voiding the ordinance, the Court opinion indicated it would be difficult to find a more effective regulation providing prior restraint than having the chief of police with such wide authority to deny. No standards were provided in the ordinance to guide the chief. It did not matter that the talks were generally considered unpopular, and that they may have interfered with people using the recreational facilities of the park, for, after all, if noisy, the noise could be controlled by "regulating decibels." And the hours and places could be regulated if the city so desired. The city could not, however, be "given the power to deny a man the use of his radio in order to protect his neighbor against sleepless nights." The Court found that loud-speakers had become "indispensable instruments of effective public speech. It is the way people are reached." One who wishes to speak need not prove that his speech will or will not annoy someone who hears it.[25]

23. *Ibid.*, 348.
24. *Saia* v. *N.Y.*, 334 U.S. 558.
25. *Ibid.*, 561, 562.

Justice Frankfurter dissented.

> The native power of human speech can interfere little
> with the self-protection of those who do not wish to
> listen. They may easily move beyond earshot. . . . But
> modern devices for amplifying the range and volume of
> the voice, or its recording, afford easy, too easy, oppor-
> tunity for aural aggression. If uncontrolled, the result is
> intrusion into cherished privacy.[26]

The year following *Saia*, the Supreme Court decided that
a Trenton, New Jersey, ordinance controlling the use of
sound trucks, sound amplifiers, and loud-speakers on the
public streets, alleys, or thoroughfares was valid. It forbad
the use of such devices if they emit "loud and raucous noises."

In *Kovacs* v. *Cooper*,[27] the Court found that the Trenton
ordinance was carefully drawn and did not have the discre-
tionary authority which was objectionable in the New York
case. Justice Reed said that the avowed purpose of the Trenton
ordinance and others similar was to prohibit or minimize
such sounds on or near the streets, since some citizens find the
noise objectionable and to some degree an interference with
the business or social activities in which they are engaged, or
the quiet they would like to enjoy. He would not go along
with a notion that the amplifier noise be kept to the noise
level of the street, since then what was amplified could not
be heard. Conversely, the unrestricted use of these devices
throughout the city would be intolerable. And "absolute
prohibition within municipal limits *of all sound amplification*,
even though reasonably regulated in place, in volume, is
undesirable, *probably unconstitutional* as an unreasonable interference with normal activities." He did not find the Trenton
ordinance one abridging freedom of speech. "It is an extrav-
agant extension of due process to say that because of it a city
cannot forbid talking on the streets through a loud speaker
in a loud and raucous tone." Although the four dissenting
justices pondered how sound trucks can be anything but loud

26. *Ibid.*, 563.
27. 336 U.S. 77 (1949).

and raucous, Justice Reed considered that the preferred position of freedom of speech did not require legislators to be insensible to claims by citizens to comfort and convenience. "To enforce freedom of speech in disregard of the rights of others would be harsh and arbitrary in itself."[28]

Different conditions faced the Supreme Court in 1951 with *Breard* v. *City of Alexandria*,[29] but it also involved the superior position of freedom of speech and press. The city had enacted a Green River Ordinance which would forbid "solicitors, peddlers, hawksters, itinerant merchants or transient vendors . . ." who go in or upon private residences to sell without having been permitted in advance to do so. There had been complaints by the citizens of the community that they had been annoyed by solicitors and that many were either undesirable or discourteous. They urged the enactment of the ordinance to prevent "any uninvited intrusion into the privacy of the home." The assumption was clear that unwanted knocks on the door by day or night were a nuisance to peace and quiet. In his opinion for the Court, Justice Reed wrote: "The Constitution's protection of property rights does not make a state or a city impotent to guard its citizens against the annoyances of life because the regulation may restrict the manner of doing legitimate business."[30] Mr. Breard sought to have the ordinance declared invalid as violating the Due Process Clause of the Fourteenth Amendment. He claimed that it did not permit a state or its subdivisions to deprive a specialist in door-to-door selling of his means of livelihood. He was not concerned that his specialists might have intruded upon the privacy of a householder who did not invite them, did not wish to see them, and did not want to hear their sales pitch. If did not matter that the solicitor might awaken a householder or otherwise disturb him by the knock or other summons.

A further claim was made by Breard that the ordinance was invalid because it interfered with interstate commerce.

28. *Ibid.*, 81, 82, 87, 88.
29. 341 U.S. 622.
30. *Ibid.*, 632.

Justice Reed did not find that claim very appealing. "Inter-state commerce itself knocks on the local door. It is only by regulating that knock that the interests of the home may be protected by the public as distinct from private action."[31]

Reed also said that the city council had a duty "of protect-ing its citizens against the practices deemed subversive of privacy and quiet. A householder depends for protection on his city board rather than churlishly guarding his entrances with orders forbidding the entrance of solicitors."[32] The suggestion that a sign outside the house declaring that no solicitors were wanted caused the justice to observe that it might have to take on billboard proportions to make the dis-tinctions between those the householder would welcome and those he would not, a scheme he found hardly acceptable. To the Court, freedom of speech and press did not mean that an individual could take or distribute where, when, and how he chose. "Rights other than those of the advocates are involved. By adjustment of rights, we can have both full liberty of expression and an orderly life."[33] The Court distinguished its decision upholding the ordinance as a protection to the right to privacy from the earlier *Struthers* case. The latter upheld the right of the free exercise of religion where there was no element of the commercial and where there was free distribution of materials. Restraints are few for the distribution of religious literature, but secular materials do not fare so well.

These cases indicate a conflict in rights. Religious materials could be distributed freely and in the same manner as Mr. Breard's solicitors, with the same path to the same door, the same door to be knocked, and the same householder to be summoned. Even though the intrusion is the same and the annoyance similar, one is sanctioned and the other is not. The distinction is "commercial." The Alexandria ordinance was settled on a balancing of the convenience between house-holders and their desire for privacy and the right of the pub-lisher to distribute. The issue "brings into collision the rights

31. *Ibid.*, 636, 637.
32. *Ibid.*, 640.
33. *Ibid.*, 642.

of the hospitable housewife, peering on Monday morning around her chained door with those of Mr. Breard's courteous, well-trained but possibly persistent solicitors. . . ." The conclusion was that the privacy of the housewife should prevail since "subscriptions may be made by anyone interested . . . without the annoyances of house to house canvassing."[34] The same might be said for religious literature.

Justice Black, strong and persistent defender of freedoms as specifically written in the Bill of Rights, took issue with the majority view in *Breard*. He felt that the preferred status of the First Amendment was put in jeopardy.

> It is my belief that the freedom of the people . . . cannot survive even a little governmental hobbling of religious or political ideas, whether they be communicated orally or through the press. The constitutional sanctuary for the press must necessarily include liberty to publish and circulate . . . , it must also include freedom to solicit paying subscribers.[35]

Even though Black's view did not prevail, the Court has given strong support to the preferred status of freedom of the press. In his famous 1941 opinion, Black said:

> Freedom to speak and write about public questions is as important to the life of our government as is the heart of the human body. In fact, this privilege is the heart of our government! If that heart is weakened, the result is debilitation; if it be stilled, the result is death.[36]

And Blackstone told us that

> the liberty of the press is indeed essential to the nature of a free state: but this consists in laying no previous restraints upon publications, and not in freedom from censure for criminal matter when published. Every freeman has an undoubted right to lay what sentiments he pleases before the public: to forbid this, is to destroy

34. *Ibid.*, 644.
35. *Ibid.*, 650.
36. *Milk Wagon Drivers Union* v. *Meadowmoor Dairies*, 312 U.S. 287, 301–302.

the freedom of the press: but if he publishes what is improper, mischievous or illegal, he must take the consequence of his own territory.[37]

Blackstone has been criticized for this view because the immunity does not exhaust the concept of the liberty guaranteed. Cooley wrote that

the mere exemption from previous restraints cannot be all that is secured by the constitutional provisions . . . [for otherwise] the liberty of the press might be rendered a mockery and a delusion, and the phrase itself a by-word, if, while every man was at liberty to publish what he pleased, the public authorities might nevertheless punish him for harmless publications.[38]

In 1964 the U.S. Supreme Court decided *Times* v. *Sullivan*.[39] At issue was whether a public official could recover damages from the *New York Times* for alleged untrue statements which were made about him and which were highly critical of his official conduct. The Court said that he could not unless he could prove that the statements published were made with actual malice. Any such statements had to be made with the knowledge that they were false and reckless to begin with and were made with complete disregard as to their falsity. The Court reiterated prior positions taken on the importance of free discussion and the need for interchange of debate on public issues. Such debate should be free and open, robust and uninhibited. Those in public life, said the Court, are a natural part of the debate and they sacrifice their privacy when they reach the "altar of public service." The constitutional guarantees of the First Amendment have supremacy in speech and press and a public official cannot claim libel unless the official offended can prove actual malice.

On June 12, 1967, the Court gave its decision in two cases involving publication claimed to violate libel laws. In *Curtis*

37. William Blackstone, *Commentaries on the Laws of England* (San Francisco; Bancroft-Whitney Co., 1890); 4:151, 152.

38. Thomas M. Cooley, *A Treatise on the Constitutional Limitations*, 8th ed. (Boston: Little, Brown & Co., 1883), 2:885.

39. 376 U.S. 254. See also, *Garrison* v. *Louisiana*, 379 U.S. 64 (1964).

Publishing Co. v. *Butts*,[40] an article in the *Saturday Evening Post* accused Butts, at the time athletic director for the University of Georgia, of conspiring to "fix" a football game between the University of Georgia and the University of Alabama, played in 1962. The facts indicated that Butts was employed by the Georgia Athletic Corporation, a private corporation, and not directly by the university.

At the trial, the jury was instructed that in order for the defense of truth to be sustained, it was necessary that the truth be substantially portrayed in those parts of the article which libeled Butts. The "sting" of the libel was said to be the charge that Butts rigged and fixed the game. The jury returned a verdict for Butts which the Court reduced substantially. *Curtis* sought a new trial which was rejected on the ground that Butts was not a public official. On appeal, the U.S. Supreme Court affirmed the verdict in favor of Butts.

The companion case involved retired U.S. Army General Edwin A. Walker,[41] and arose out of a news dispatch about a riot on the night of September 30, 1962, on the University of Mississippi campus which erupted when federal authorities made efforts to enforce the enrollment of a Negro, James A. Meredith. Walker, who was present on the campus, was reported to have taken command of the violent crowd and led them in a charge against the federal officials. The report also claimed that Walker encouraged the rioters to use violence. Incidentally, he had been in command of the federal troops at Little Rock, Arkansas, in 1957 in connection with the school desegregation problem.

Walker sought damages in the Texas courts. The Associated Press which had sent out the report raised the defense of truth and constitutional defenses. The jury was instructed that an award of compensatory damages could be made if the dispatch was not substantially true, and that punitive damages could be added if the article was actuated by ill will, bad or evil motive, or "that entire want of care in its preparation was determined." The verdict was for $500,000 compensatory

40. 388 U.S. 130.
41. *Ibid.*, 140.

damages and $300,000 punitive damages. But the judge
refused to enter the award. He noted a lack of malice if the
ruling in *New York Times* was applicable.[42] The Texas Court
of Appeals affirmed the award for compensatory damages
and found *New York Times* not applicable.

The U.S. Supreme Court determined that Walker was not
a public official and could recover "on a showing of highly
unreasonable conduct constituting an extreme departure from
the standards of investigating and reporting ordinarily adhered
to by responsible publishers."[43] But in comparing *Walker* to
Butts, the Court said that "considering the necessity for rapid
dissemination, nothing in this series of events gives the
slightest hint of a severe departure," and concluded that
General Walker was not entitled to damages from the Associated Press.[44] To dispel any concern about the companion
Butts case, the Court said:

> ... where a publisher's departure from standards of
> responsibility is severe enough to strip from him the
> constitutional protection our decision acknowledges, we
> think it entirely proper for the State to act not only for the
> protection of the individual injured but to safeguard all
> those similarly situated against like abuse.[45]

In a related case, Marvin L. Pickering, a teacher in a high
school in Illinois, was dismissed from his position by the
Board of Education for sending a letter which was printed
in a local newspaper concerning school financing, and was

42. *Ibid.*, 142.
43. *Ibid.*, 155.
44. *Ibid.*, 159.
45. *Ibid.*, 161. On April 29, 1968, in *St. Amant* v. *Thompson*, the
U.S. Supreme Court referred to the *New York Times* case saying that
to be subjected to damages for publication there must be proof of
"reckless disregard" for the defamatory statements made about a
public official and whether the publisher had serious doubts as to
the truth of what was published. "Publishing with such doubts shows
reckless disregard for truth or falsity and demonstrates actual
malice." The opinion sought to distinguish between some erroneous
publications and some true ones, those protected and those which
are not.

critical of the school superintendent and the board. The board considered the letter "detrimental to the efficient operation and administration of the schools of the district." Pickering claimed his First and Fourteenth Amendment rights had been violated. The Illinois trial court agreed with the board and the Supreme Court of Illinois affirmed.

But the U.S. Supreme Court reversed. In an opinion by Justice Marshall, the Court said that the statements made by Pickering were "in no way directed towards any person with whom appellant would normally be in contact in the course of his daily work as a teacher." Nor did the statements impede the teacher's "proper performance of his daily duties in the classroom or to have interfered with the regular operation of the schools generally."

In conclusion, Marshall said, "We hold that, in a case such as this, absent proof of false statements knowingly or recklessly made by him, a teacher's exercise of his right to speak on issues of public importance may not furnish the basis for his dismissal from public employment." The record indicated, however, that some of the statements were actually false.[46]

A public official may not have much claim to a right to privacy when claimed invasions relate to the conduct of his office, but to what extent do private lives have protection against the supremacy of the freedom to publish? It has been observed that urbanization of society has produced many forces which intrude upon personal privacy. We live in close proximity to countless others. We walk on crowded streets, ride on crowded buses, subways, and drive bumper to bumper even on major throughways. Few of us are able to remain very long in isolation from others, and what one of us does likely affects others to some degree. In this crowded complex there are those whose livelihood depends upon inquiry into what we do, what we think, the kind of life we lead. These take various forms of being newsworthy, and the media have insatiable appetites. We may not know when or under what circumstances we may blink at the unexpected flash of a

46. *Pickering* v. *Board of Education*, ——— U.S. ———.

news photographer's camera or read in a newspaper or hear on radio or television of some activity we considered private and personal and not the business of the world at large. This is not to suggest that all news media inquiries and publications are invasions of personal privacy, but some embarrass and annoy, some may mean loss of status, friends, and even economic well-being. But the freedom of the press demands a high degree of latitude so that the "free state" can continue.

The Federal Reporter for 1940 includes a case involving the publication of an article in the *New Yorker* magazine about a child prodigy who in later life went into obscurity. The federal Court upheld the right of the publisher over the claim of the chief character that his privacy had been invaded. In 1910, William James Sidis was well publicized, primarily because at age eleven he lectured to a group of distinguished mathematicians and at age sixteen was graduated from Harvard College. But soon thereafter little public notice was given about him. In 1937, according to the magazine article, he had sought to live in obscurity in a shabby area of Boston, and was employed as an "insignificant clerk." It recorded Sidis' efforts and passion for privacy and the lengths to which he had gone to avoid public scrutiny. The Court did not decide against Sidis without some sympathy.[47] But it found he was once a public figure and of him "great deeds were expected." The public was entitled to know whether he had fulfilled the promise expected of him and therefore his life was still a matter of public concern.

The U.S. Supreme Court had occasion in 1967 to consider whether a family had been wronged by the freedom of the press in the reporting of a false account of the family's experience in being held by fugitives from justice.[48] A New York court awarded damages in a jury trial against Time, Inc., publishers of *Life* magazine, which had published the article

47. *Sidis* v. *F-R Pub. Co.* 113 F 2d, 806, 809. Cited in Harry Kalven, Jr., "Privacy in Tort Law—Were Warren and Brandeis Wrong?", *Law and Contemporary Problems* 31, no. 2 (Spring 1966):337.

48. *Time, Inc.* v. *Hill*, 385 U.S. 374. Richard M. Nixon of New York was counsel for Hill.

on a play containing circumstances which identified the Hill family in effect. Hill claimed it untrue and that the writer and publisher knew it was untrue. Involved was a New York "right to privacy" statute.

The U.S. Supreme Court reversed the lower court action. It seems that Hill and his family were held in their home against their will by escaped convicts for some nineteen hours, and this became front-page news; but the claim against Time, Inc., was the article about a piece of fiction which was alleged to be actually about the Hill family except that Hill claimed the experiences related were false.

The Court had already decided *New York Times* involving a public official. *Time, Inc.* v. *Hill* was different, but the outcome was the same. The concurring opinion by Justice Douglas best presents the tenor of the Court's decision.

> A fictionalized treatment of the event is, in my view, as much in the public domain as would be a water color of the assassination of a public official. It seems to me irrelevant to talk of any right of privacy in this context. Here a person is catapulted into the news by events over which he has no control. He and his activities are then in the public domain as fully as the matters at issue in *New York Times v. Sullivan*. Such privacy as a person normally has ceases when his life ceases to be private.[49]

Justice Black also concurred. As might be expected, he supported freedom of the press over any position of personal privacy. He thought that if there was an error in reporting it was an understandable error in the reporting of a newsworthy event. Speaking of the jury award which was being reversed, he wrote:

> One does not have to be a prophet to foresee that judgments like the one we here reverse can frighten the press so much that publishers will cease trying to report the

49. *Ibid.*, 401. For a discussion of the two cases, see Dwayne Oglesby, "Freedom of the Press v. The Right of the Individual—A Continuing Controversy," *Oregon Law Review* 47, no. 2 (February 1968):132–145. He says that the facts in the two cases are too different for Hill not to have enjoyed proper constitutional safeguards. After all, *Life* had ample time to determine whether the story was true, but did not.

news in a lively and readable fashion as long as there is—
and there always will be—doubt as to the complete
accuracy of the newsworthy facts.[50]

Black was as critical of the notion of a "right" to privacy
as he was in his dissent in *Griswold*. He felt that if a right to
privacy had been created by judges in *Hill* (New York had
done it by statute), then could they not create other rights
as time passed? He found that the First Amendment was
written deliberately in the language stated and "put its
freedoms beyond the reach of government to change it while it
remained unrepealed."[51]

Justice Fortas wrote a lengthy dissent. It is a sturdy support
for personal privacy and a forceful position against the
majority, one defending the judicial view that there is a
fundamental right to privacy derived from the Bill of Rights.
He gave strong emphasis to the place of privacy.

> I do not believe the First Amendment precludes effective
> protection of the right of privacy—or, for that matter, an
> effective law of libel. . . . There are great and important
> values in our society, none of which is greater than those
> reflected in the First Amendment, but which are also
> fundamental and entitled to this Court's careful respect
> and protection. Among these is the right to privacy, which
> has been eloquently extolled by scholars and members
> of this Court.[52]

Justice Fortas then traced the development of this "right"
from Cooley's *Torts*, the Warren-Brandeis article on privacy,[53]
and a series of U.S. Supreme Court cases which gave recogni-

50. *Time, Inc.* v. *Hill*, 400, 401.
51. *Ibid.*, 400.
52. *Ibid.*, 412.
53. *Ibid.* It should be noted that Fortas begins his résumé with
Cooley, not the Warren-Brandeis article. Other decisions begin with
Warren-Brandeis. Reference to Cooley's "right to be alone" appears
early in the article. The Supreme Court recognized Cooley's contribution in *Adair* v. *U.S.*, 208 U.S. 161 (1908). "It is a part of every
man's civil rights that he be left at liberty to refuse business relations
with any person whomsoever, whether the refusal rests upon reason,
or is the result of whim, caprice, prejudice or malice. With his

tion to privacy as a right. He especially cited the case of *Mapp* v. *Ohio* to say that the Court had referred to the right to privacy, a right "no less important than any other right carefully and particularly reserved to the people." He found, he wrote, that a distinct right of privacy "is now recognized" either as a common law right or by statute in at least thirty-five states. The right to privacy is, "simply stated, the right to be left alone; to live one's life as one chooses, free from assault, intrusion or invasion except as they can be justified by the clear needs of community living under a government of law." [54]

To Fortas, a public official such as Sullivan is fair game for publicity; but a private person and his family, imposed upon by escaped convicts, held in their home in fear of their lives, and whose experiences were falsely reported should have recourse. He could not understand why the Court should not support the right of a state to provide a remedy for reckless "falsity in writing and publishing an article which irresponsibly and injuriously invades the privacy of a quiet family for no purpose except dramatic interest and commercial appeal." It appears from the case that the writers of the article for *Life* had adequate time to find out the facts had they wanted to do so.

The freedoms guaranteed in the First Amendment have been given the stamp of supremacy many times, and when in conflict with other rights, including the derivative right to privacy, the amendment's rights remain generally supreme over any other rights. Freedom of religious practice appears to dominate all others, and freedom of speech and press may suffer because of the old clear and present danger or the more recent bad tendency tests, but they do not suffer much with any attempts at prior restraint.

---

reasons neither the public nor third persons have any legal concern." What to Cooley was a right, the right to be let alone, to refuse relations with others regardless of reasons of it, has become a denial of that right. *Brown* v. *Board of Education of Topeka*, 347 U.S. 483 (1954).

54. *Time Inc.* v. *Hill*, 413.

But does freedom of speech include freedom of silence? During the last several years the issue of the right to silence has been tested before the U.S. Supreme Court, especially in the "Fifth Amendment Cases" arising from contempt citations by the Committee on Un-American Activities. It is not intended here to review the issues or history of those controversies except to indicate in selected instances how the High Court has dealt with the problem as it relates to the privacy of silence.

In the 1957 *Watkins* case,[55] the Court said that the committee could not engage in exposure for the sake of exposure, and appeared to say that there was really no recognized definition of what was un-American, except one so vague that it could not be a proper purpose for a legislative investigative committee. This decision was widely supported by critics of the committee who felt it frequently went beyond constitutional guarantees in virtually forcing "speech" when those before it considered "silence" an equal right. To remain silent or to "take the Fifth" frequently meant a contempt citation.

The hope of the critics was short-lived. In 1959, the Court decided *Barenblatt* v. *U.S.*[56] Lloyd Barenblatt, at the time he was asked to appear before the committee, was a teacher at Vassar, but at the time he answered his summons his contract had expired and he was not employed. He was called before the committee because he had been identified by an ex-Communist as an active participant in Communist causes while he was a student and teacher at the University of Michigan. At the hearing, he refused to answer questions. He chose silence.

In his opinion for the majority, Justice Harlan summed up the issue in these words. "We conclude that the balance between the individual and the governmental interests here at stake must be struck in favor of the latter, and that therefore the provisions of the First Amendment have not been offen-

55. *Watkins* v. *U.S.* 354 U.S. 178.
56. 360 U.S. 109.

ded."[57] It may have been of no comfort to Barenblatt, but Justice Black sharply dissented.

> To apply the Court's balancing test under such circumstances is to have the First Amendment to say "Congress shall pass no law abridging freedom of speech, press, assembly and petition, unless Congress and the Supreme Court reach a joint conclusion that on balance the interest of the Government in stifling these freedoms is greater than the interests of the people in having them exercised."[58]

The right to silence before a state legislative investigating committee received support, however, in *Gibson* v. *Florida Investigating Committee* in 1963.[59] It upheld the closely related claim of "associational privacy."

The Florida committee sought to obtain the entire membership list of the Miami branch of the National Association for the Advancement of Colored People. The local director declined to produce the list. He said he would answer questions based on his own personal knowledge as members of the committee might ask, but no more. In reviewing his conviction, the U.S. Supreme Court conceded the right of the State of Florida to inform itself through its legislature, but it found no tie between the NAACP and the quest for locating subversion.

In the majority opinion, Justice Goldberg supported the right to privacy. Rights of association "are within the ambit of the constitutional protections afforded by the First and Fourteenth Amendments. And it is equally clear that the guarantee encompasses protection of privacy of association in organizations such as that of which the petitioner is president."[60] Goldberg also said that it was not Communists the committee was seeking, it was the NAACP itself which was the subject of the investigation. Justice Douglas concurred with these comments:

> There is no other course consistent with the Free Society invisioned by the First Amendment. For the views a

57. *Ibid.*, 134.   58. *Ibid.*, 143.
59. 372 U.S. 539 (1963).   60. *Ibid.*, 544.

citizen entertains, the beliefs he harbors, the utterances he makes, the ideology he embraces and the people he associates with are no concern of government. That article of faith marks, indeed, the main difference between the Free Society which we espouse and the dictatorships both on the Left and the Right.[61]

In 1966 the Court was asked to reverse a conviction in an Ohio case[62] because the prosecution commented on the failure of the defendant to testify. The Court reaffirmed its decision in *Mapp* that the defendant did not have to testify and there could not be any adverse comment about it. Justice Stewart wrote some pertinent comments about the right to privacy and the right to be silent. He said that the basic purpose of a trial is a determination of truth, but

> by contrast, the Fifth Amendment's privilege against self-incrimination is not an adjunct to the ascertainment of truth. That privilege, like the guarantee of the Fourth Amendment, stands as a protection of quite different constitutional values—values reflecting the concern of our society for the right of each individual to be let alone.[63]

Even so, the defendant lost. The justice said that to require all states to "void the conviction of every person who did not testify at his own trial would have an impact upon the administration of their criminal laws so devastating as to need no elaboration." The retroactive application of newer rules was not to be enforced.

Is there a right to be silent? Wigmore in *Evidence* says that

> from the point of view of society's *right* to our testimony, it is to be remembered that the demand comes, not from any one person or set of persons, but from the community as a whole,—from justice as an institution, and from law and order as indispensable elements of civilized life.[64]

61. *Ibid.*, 570.
62. *Tehan* v. *Shott*, 382 U.S. 406.
63. *Ibid.*, 416.
64. John Henry Wigmore, *A Treatise on the Anglo-American System of Evidence in Trials at Common Law*, 3d ed. (Boston: Little, Brown & Co., 1940), 8:66.

Most people believe, however, that if one is requested to appear and testify before a grand jury proceeding, a legislative committee, or in a court, he has an obligation to do so whether his privacy is invaded or not. Because the need for information which can come from those asked to make these appearances is so great in the interest of justice, many states and the U.S. government have provided immunity from prosecution if they testify. The view is that justice will be served better if he who testifies avoids jail than not to have the testimony.

It is one thing to say that a person appearing to give testimony has an obligation and quite another that he must give testimony. The prior cases upholding the right to remain silent were given added status in two 1967 decisions. These were *Spevack* v. *Klein*[65] and *Garrity* v. *New Jersey*.[66]

The *Spevack* case involved a state law providing that if certain state officials and employees refused to answer questions of any authorized official agency on the grounds of self-incrimination they would be removed from office or employment. Spevack was an attorney, and an effort was made to disbar him for the alleged misconduct, that is, his failure to testify. The Court said, in affirming *Malloy*,[67] that the Fourteenth Amendment guarantees the right of a person to remain silent unless he chooses to speak "in the unfettered exercise of his own will, and to suffer no penalty . . . for such silence."[68] Justice Douglas also concluded that lawyers enjoy first-class citizenship.

The companion *Garrity* case involved a traffic-fixing investigation. The policemen involved were advised that they could refuse to answer questions, but if they did they would be removed from their jobs. Here, too, the Court observed that policemen are not relegated to a "watered-down version of constitutional rights."[69]

65. 385 U.S. 511.
66. 385 U.S. 493.
67. 385 U.S. 511, 514; 378 U.S. 1, 8 (1964).
68. 385 U.S., 514.
69. 385 U.S. 493, 500. In his concurring opinion in *Garrity*, Justice Fortas distinguishes it from *Spevack*. "This Court has never held, for

It seems reasonable to conclude that the right to silence
will be recognized, without force or penalty, but probably
not in national security cases. If this is the prevailing doctrine,
it will likely mean that a witness granted immunity will
receive careful treatment from officials to ensure that immunity
is actually granted and not circumvented by reason of incriminating statements or resulting evidence, or for any other
reason.

---

example, that a policeman may not be discharged for refusal in dis-
ciplinary proccedings to testify as to his conduct as a police officer.
It is quite a different matter if the State seeks to use the testimony
given under this lash in a criminal proceeding," 519, 520. See
also, Michael Franck, "The Myth of *Spevack* v. *Klein*," *American
Bar Association Journal* 54 (October 1968):970–974. Franck interprets
the Fortas explanation to mean that a public employee could be
discharged for refusing to answer on the scope of his responsibilities,
but not an attorney. As Fortas put it, "A lawyer is not an employee
of the State." He suggests that the employee has a greater responsibility to the states *as an employee* than does a lawyer.

IV

Well-Ordered Liberty

Privacy rights have long been in contest with the police power of the states. Restraints upon individual private activity are many and varied, but they find their constitutional base in the ill-defined and often vague references to the power of the state, through its legislature, both to restrain and promote in the search for the common good.

Early in this century, the U.S. Supreme Court had this to say about the exercise of that governmental authority.

> Another vital principle is that, except as restrained by its own fundamental law, or by the Supreme Law of the Land, a state possesses all legislative power consistent with a republican form of government; therefore each State, when not thus restrained and so far as this court is concerned, may, by legislation, provide not only for the health, morals, and safety of its people, but for the common good, as involved in the well-being, peace, happiness, and prosperity of the people.[1]

The legislative power of the state, therefore, embraces those regulations which have as their stated purpose and design to promote the public convenience or the general prosperity and also those to promote and secure the public safety, health, and morals. It is not a solely negative power, not being confined to the suppression of what may be considered offensive, disorderly, unsafe, or unsanitary, but

1. *Halter* v. *Nebraska*, 205 U.S. 34, 40, 41 (1907).

includes that which is determined to be for the greatest welfare of the people.

In a 1914 decision, the U.S. Supreme Court said, in construing the police power, that it was the power of the state "to establish all regulations that are reasonably necessary to secure the health, safety, good order, comfort, or general welfare of the community; that this power can be neither abdicated nor bargained away, and is inalienable even by express grant."[2]

It is a free-wheeling power and apparently not subject to limitation as long as the means employed to carry out the authority is not arbitrary nor oppressive and bears directly on the subjects stated: the public health, public safety, public morals, or some of the other phases of the general welfare.[3] Thus, the legislatures of the fifty states can and do provide regulations through statutes and ordinances which may invade the liberty of individuals thereby and declare many acts unlawful and punishable. As Justice Cardozo put it in his opinion in *Palko* v. *Connecticut* in 1937, the states are free to adopt any standards as long as they are not in conflict with the concept of ordered liberty and did not violate principles of justice so rooted in the traditions and conscience of the people as to be ranked as fundamental.[4]

It is the purpose of this chapter to relate a number of subjects included within the police power which have imposed restraints on freedom of personal action, have interfered with privacy, or curtail or prevent individual choices and practices. It is not intended to argue that they are right or wrong, but rather only to show the nature of interference with privacy. It is liberty and freedom within limits; it is the right to privacy up to a point. It is liberty and freedom based upon legis-

2. *Atlantic Coast Line R. Co.* v. *Goldsboro*, 232 U.S. 548, 558.

3. *Treigle* v. *Acme Homestead Assoc.*, 297 U.S. 189, 197 (1936); *Liggett* v. *Baldridge*, 278 U.S. 105, 111–112 (1928).

4. 302 U.S. 319, 325. In this case, Justice Cardozo presented his "honor roll" of rights, indicating some rights have a higher value than others, and that some properly belong in the Fourteenth Amendment.

lative determination and judicial interpretation of social order and the social good. The police power assumes that the restraints are essential to "the orderly pursuit of happiness by free men."[5]

Many governmental regulations imposed under the police power relate to morals. Some result from a conflict with other rights, such as between religious practices and doctrines and claims to privacy. Others have been enacted to help ensure public safety and the health of a community or of the state. Still others have roots in the promotion of the general welfare.

One of the earliest privacy cases to come before the U.S. Supreme Court involved a U.S. statute for the Territories which prohibited plural marriages. The claim was that the practice of polygamy was wholly within the bounds of freedom of religion. The United States took the position that polygamy had no place in a civilized society and could not be protected under any claim of the First Amendment, and that the Territorial Act was in no way an abridgment of freedom of religion.

Reynolds v. *U.S.* was decided in 1878.[6] Eighty-seven years later came *Griswold*. In the latter, the opinion of the Court finished with these words:

> We deal with a right of privacy older than the Bill of
> Rights—older than our political parties, older than our

5. *Meyer* v. *Nebraska*, 262 U.S. 390, 399 (1923). For a discussion showing conflicting views of the proper role for society in regulating or imposing morality, see the exchange between Patrick A. D. Devlin, *The Enforcement of Morals* (London: Oxford, 1965), and H. L. A. Hart, *Law, Liberty and Morality* (Stanford: Stanford Univ. Press, 1963). Lord Devlin takes the position that immorality may be something which can jeopardize a society's existence, and to preserve it society has the right to enforce a morals code. Hart's view is that practices condemned by some members of society but which do not harm other persons should be outside the realm of law. The U.S. Supreme Court in the recent decision in *Stanley* v. *Georgia*, ——— U.S. ———, involving the possession of alleged obscene movie films, supports Hart's position.

6. 98 U.S. 145. This arose in the Territory of Utah. Prior to statehood, Congress had power to enact statutes under Art. IV, Sec. 3 of the Constitution.

school system. Marriage is a coming together for better or for worse, hopefully enduring and intimate to the degree of being sacred. It is any association that promotes a way of life, not causes; a harmony in living, not political faiths; a bilateral loyalty, not commercial or social projects. Yet it is an association for as noble a purpose as any involved in our prior decisions.[7]

It is far-fetched, perhaps absurd, to assume that Justice Douglas would include plural marriages as being within the right of privacy he supported, but if marriage has such a superior position, to be protected from governmental intrusion, why did polygamy fail?

In *Reynolds*, no mention is made of any right to privacy. The discussion is about religion. "The word 'religion' is not defined in the Constitution. We must go elsewhere, therefore, to ascertain its meaning."[8] This excursion wound up with a quotation from Thomas Jefferson. "I shall see with sincere satisfaction the progress of those sentiments which tend to restore men to all his natural rights, convinced he has no natural right in opposition to his social duties."[9]

Plural marriage, said the Court, was contrary to social duty and could not be supported. The opinion roamed wide to rid the Territory of polygamy.

> Polygamy has always been odious among the northern and western nations of Europe, and until the establishment of the Mormon Church, was almost exclusively a feature of the Asiatic and African people. At common law, a second marriage was always void, and from the earliest history of England polygamy has been treated as an offence against society. . . . We think it safely may be said that there has never been a time in any State of the Union when polygamy has not been an offence against society. . . . Marriage, while from its very nature a sacred obligation, is nevertheless, in most civilized nations, a civil contract, and usually regulated by law.[10]

7. 381 U.S. 479, 486 (1965).
8. 98 U.S. 145, 162.
9. *Ibid.*, 164.
10. *Ibid.*, 164, 165.

A religious practice and doctrine, that is, plural marriage, however superior a right marriage might be, was an offense. The decisive factor in the opinion went: ". . . those who do not make polygamy a part of their religious belief may be found guilty and punished, while those who do, must be acquitted and go free." Such a dual standard could not be accepted; furthermore, "Congress, in 1862, saw fit to make bigamy a crime in the Territories. This was done because of the evil consequences that were supposed to flow from plural marriages."[11]

A few years later a case involving a state statute against the practice of polygamy permitted the Court to elaborate further. "Few crimes are more pernicious to the best interests of society. . . . It was never intended . . . that the [First] amendment could be invoked as a protection against legislation for the punishment of acts inimical to the peace, good order, and morals of society."[12]

The well-ordered society is sometimes liberal with claims to privacy. An early case in Iowa illustrates the point.[13]

Marvin moved to Iowa and brought Lucy Stone with him. According to the facts in the case, he was not married to her. Witnesses in the trial quoted him as saying he hired her to do his cooking, washing, and housework. He was told by one witness that he could not live with Lucy, for the laws of the country would not permit it. Marvin reportedly replied that "if they made a fuss about it he could marry her, and he intimated that if he wanted to have illicit intercourse with her it was his own business."[14]

Another witness was Lucy's husband. He stated that Marvin and Lucy lived together "as a hired girl to a man." He said

11. *Ibid.*, 166, 168. See also, C. Peter Magrath, "Chief Justice Waite and the 'Twin Relic': *Reynolds* v. *U.S.*," *Vanderbilt Law Review* 18, no. 2 (March 1965):507–543. Dean Magrath states that the *Reynolds* case is the leading constitutional precedent on the free exercise clause of the First Amendment.

12. *Davis* v. *Beason*, 133 U.S. 333, 341, 342 (1890).

13. *Iowa* v. *Martin*, 12 Iowa 499 (1861).

14. *Ibid.*, 503.

he had lived with Marvin and Lucy and he saw Marvin "get out of the bed with Lucy only twice, and that was when it was so cold he could not sleep upon the floor."[15] According to the Iowa Supreme Court, this was all of the evidence introduced at the trial.

In the opinion, the Iowa Court said that Lucy Stone and Marvin were living together in the same house and in the relation of master and servant and not as husband and wife. Furthermore, went the opinion, no matter what went on in the house

> secret acts of intercourse would not make them liable. The burden of the events is the open, lewd, lascivious conduct of the parties living together as husband and wife. It is the publicity and disgrace, the demoralizing and debasing influence, that the law is designed to prevent . . . the state fails to show any lascivious or indecent conduct except it is the fact of Defendant twice leaving the bed of Lucy. Whether this was in the night or in the morning, whether it was done openly or secretly the evidence fails to show.[16]

The well-ordered society subjects the individual to varying kinds of invasion of the person.[17] Some of these have been called "blood-letting" cases because blood tests were involved. Some of them concern the public safety and others the general health of the community. Others have no relation to criminal matters. Of this last group is *Cortese* v. *Cortese*.[18]

Mrs. Cortese sought support for herself and her child, who was born five months after her marriage. She admitted pre-marital relations with her husband and another man within probable limits of conception, but Mr. Cortese claimed he did not know about the other man until some fifteen months after the child's birth when she taunted him in a dispute that he was not the child's father. At that point he left her.

15. *Ibid.*
16. *Ibid.*
17. Such as *Rochin*, discussed in Chapter II.
18. 76 A 2d 717 (1950).

As a defense, Mr. Cortese sought to have Mrs. Cortese and the child submit to a blood test as provided in a state statute covering paternity cases. She refused to submit, claiming it would violate her right of personal privacy. The court did not agree with her.

> The value of blood tests as a wholesome aid in the quest for truth in the administration of justice . . . cannot be gainsaid in this day. Their reliability as an indicator of the truth has been fully recognized. The substantial weight of medical and legal authority attests their accuracy, not to prove paternity, and not always to disprove it, but they can disprove it conclusively in a great many cases.[19]

Apparently the court believed that a refusal would be sustained in a criminal case, but not in a civil case as the one being decided. The reason was that in the section of the statute involving criminal matters, the privilege was mentioned, but it was not mentioned or implied in the section applicable to civil cases.

> This omission cannot have been accidental; it is presumed to have been a matter of legislative design. It is apparent the omission reflects a legislative intent that in civil actions the trial court . . . shall have authority to order the tests despite a refusal voluntarily to submit.[20]

In another paternity case, a slightly different situation arose. The physician analyzing the blood stated categorically that it was biologically impossible for the defendant to have been the father of the child, but the jury chose to ignore his testimony. In approving the jury action, the judge said, "We cannot say that their finding is manifestly wrong."[21]

Under the authority of the police power, the states and their local subdivisions have enacted statutes and ordinances in quantity designed to protect the safety of the people. These range wide, especially as they affect property, such as buildings to provide worker or customer safety, but the public

19. *Ibid.*, 719.
20. *Ibid.*, 721.
21. *Jordan* v. *Davis*, 57 A 2d 209, 211 (1948).

safety relating to the use of motor vehicles provides for a continuous invasion of the privacy of the person.

Just as blood tests are used in paternity cases, such tests have a history of many years in determining whether the driver of an automobile may have operated it while intoxicated. In an Ohio case, one Gatton was convicted of operating a motor vehicle while under the influence of alcohol.[22] After his arrest and confinement he was asked to submit to a blood test or a urinalysis to determine alcoholic content. He refused. At the trial, this fact of refusal was admitted in testimony, and Gatton claimed that the jury was urged to consider his refusal in making its decision. He claimed this violated his constitutional rights. The court did not agree, saying that the evidence, that is, the refusal, was offered by the prosecutor, who had the right to comment thereupon, "in reasonable limits," and invaded none of the defendant's rights. After all, said the court, the evidence was not required to be disclosed by the defendant.

And as if to suggest future debate on invasions of privacy, especially rights against self-incrimination and rights to remain silent, the judge had this to say:

> There has been an increasing tendency in recent years upon the part of courts of many jurisdictions to extend the scope of the self-incrimination constitutional provisions to entirely unwarranted lengths. Modern-day transportation, which enables criminals to travel with great rapidity from one part of the state to another, or from one state to another state, together with improvements in lethal instruments, has made the path of the law-enforcement officer exceedingly rough; and it seems to the members of this court to be high time to discontinue such an attitude toward those accused of criminal offenses, and to secure to them such rights as are clearly guaranteed by the constitutional provisions, but no more.[23]

If the good justice is still living, he must have long since been raging in opposition to the protections given to those

22. *State* v. *Gatton*, 20 N.E. 2d 265 (1938).
23. *Ibid.*, 266, 267.

accused of criminal offenses by the restraints imposed upon law enforcement officials to "secure to them such rights as are clearly guaranteed."

It is quite natural for a person charged with intoxication while driving an automobile to object to having a blood test if he had been drinking. Whether he should be forced to submit and, if so, whether his privacy has been invaded is the question.

In *People* v. *Tucker*[24] the defendant was charged with violating the Motor Vehicle Code by driving while under the influence of intoxicating liquor. In the statement of facts it was claimed he drove on the wrong side of the highway and caused injury to others. After being taken into custody, and at the suggestion of a highway patrolman, a physician took a sample of Tucker's blood. At the trial the physician stated he doubted that Tucker knew he took the sample and also doubted that he even talked to him about it. Tucker was either in shock or injured so that he was not in complete control of his senses, although the physician said Tucker did as he was asked.

The blood analysis indicated that Tucker was intoxicated as defined in the Code. Tucker, at the trial, objected to the use of the physician's testimony as to the alcoholic content of the blood specimen, claiming it was a violation of his rights, since it was taken without his knowledge or consent. The state supreme court did not agree. The ruling was that the trial court was not wrong in admitting the evidence, and Tucker's rights had not been violated.

Because of its importance in the search and seizure cases, the 1952 case involving the stomach pumping of Antonio Richard Rochin was presented in Chapter II.[25] But it belongs here also considering the desire of the state of California to control or rid itself of what it considered an undesirable and socially evil practice: the ultimate consumption of narcotics. Rochin was convicted on the charge of possessing a preparation of morphine in violation of the California Health and

24. 198 P 2d 941 (1948).
25. 342 U.S. 165.

Safety Code. There was no doubt about possession of the drug: it was taken from his stomach. Two judges of the Supreme Court of California dissented in that stage of the judicial treatment of the case, saying they "found no valid ground of distinction between a verbal confession extracted by physical abuse and a confession wrested from defendant's body by physical abuse." [26]

In the course of the opinion of the U.S. Supreme Court, Justice Frankfurter upheld Rochin's right to personal privacy. He found the manner in which the evidence was produced was "conduct that shocks the conscience." He referred to "illegally breaking into the privacy of the petitioner, the struggle to open his mouth and remove what was there, the forcible extraction of his stomach's contents . . . is bound to offend even hardened sensibilities." [27]

Five years later the Supreme Court made a nice distinction between the forcible taking of a stomach's contents and the forcible taking of blood. In *Breithaupt* v. *Abram* [28] the majority opinion by Justice Clark stated that the taking of blood by a skilled technician was not conduct that would shock the conscience, nor would it offend any sense of justice. In this case a licensed physician drew a sample of blood and the laboratory analysis showed an alcohol content above the minimum defined for a state of nonintoxication. The defendant objected to having the results of the test presented at the trial. Said Clark:

> The individual's right to immunity from such invasion of the body as is involved in a properly safeguarded blood test is far outweighed by the value of its deterrent affect due to public realization that the issue of driving while under the influence of alcohol can often by this method be taken out of the confusion of conflicting contentions. [29]

Breithaupt was unconscious when the blood sample was taken. He had no opportunity to consent or object. But Clark

26. *Ibid.*, 167, citing 101 Calif. App. 2d 143.
27. *Ibid.*, 172.
28. 352 U.S. 432 (1957).
29. *Ibid.*, 439, 440.

thought that this was not brutal or offensive because it was done under the protective eye of the licensed physician. He agreed that it was taken while the defendant was in no position to object, but "the absence of conscious consent, without more, does not necessarily render the taking a violation of a constitutional right; and certainly the test as administered here would not be considered offensive by even the most delicate."[30] He found that the blood test procedure had become routine in everyday life, even though it might be claimed that the taking of the blood was against the right of an individual that his person be held inviolable. He also observed that blood tests were a common event for millions of Americans.[31] He placed the practice and the possible right of an individual that his person be held inviolable against the interests of society, that is, the safety on the roads. "And the more so since the test likewise may establish innocence, thus affording protection against the treachery of judgment based on one or more of the senses."[32]

Chief Justice Warren dissented, pointing out that apparently the forcible taking of the blood for the intoxication test was no violation unless force was used. He considered this a serious breach of rights if it rested on the question of whether physical resistance of a suspect was necessary as a condition of establishing rights.

It might be concluded from *Rochin* and *Breithaupt* that in the former the Court majority considered the injury to society less severe if the stomach were left inviolate, but in the latter society needed the scientific proof, not judgments of eyewitnesses, to try to eliminate the slaughter caused by drunken drivers. Chief Justice Warren, joined by Justices Black and Douglas, dissenting in *Breithaupt*, thought that

> due process means that at least that law-enforcement officers in their efforts to obtain evidence from persons suspected of crime must stop short of bruising the body,

30. *Ibid.*, 435, 436.
31. *Ibid.*, 436.
32. *Ibid.*, 439.

breaking the skin, puncturing tissue or extracting body fluids, whether they contemplate doing it by force or stealth. [33]

Several years earlier in an Idaho case,[34] the state supreme court was faced with an issue similar to *Breithaupt*. Ayres was convicted of involuntary manslaughter caused while driving his automobile. While he was unconscious after the accident, blood was taken from his arm and tested. The test showed that he was not legally intoxicated. This information was presented during the trial and he objected to its introduction. The state court said that Ayres had nothing to complain about. He did not introduce the evidence which was favorable to him—the prosecution did—and there was no basis for sustaining any objection that it should not have been presented.

These invasions of the right of the individual to have his person protected were not enhanced in a 1966 case[35] which affirmed the decision in *Breithaupt*. In *Schmerber* v. *California* the majority opinion in the U.S. Supreme Court held there was nothing self-incriminating in the forcible taking of a blood sample for a test if done in a medical setting. The only objection which could be sustained, said Justice Brennan, would be from the use of physical or moral compulsion to get the evidence. Justice Black, dissenting, as did the chief justice and Justices Douglas and Fortas, said "To reach the conclusions that compelling a person to give his blood to help the State convict him is not equivalent to compelling him to be a witness against himself strikes me as quite an extraordinary feat."[36]

In a Maryland case[37] the question was presented whether evidence could be introduced after objection that a blood sample taken was the same blood type on a murder victim's clothes and the defendant's clothes. The defendant claimed he had been in a fight with two men at the time of the murder

33. *Ibid.*, 442.
34. *State* v. *Ayres*, 211 P 2d 142 (1949).
35. 384 U.S. 757.
36. *Ibid.*, 773.
37. *Davis* v. *State*, 57 A 2d 289 (1948).

and the blood type of one of them was the same as that found on his sleeve. The blood on the sleeve of the defendant's coat could have come from either the victim or the man with the same blood type with whom he had been fighting. Whether it was or not, the defendant claimed the state had no right to take his blood—and by subterfuge—and use it against him. The Maryland court had this to say:

> Many courts have held that an accused in a criminal case may be compelled to give a specimen of his blood, and that this is within the inherent judicial power. Other jurisdictions hold a contrary position. . . . We do not here have to decide this question. What is before us is the admissibility of evidence. . . . There is no substantial difference between obtaining a specimen of blood from an accused and obtaining his fingerprints, physical property, the possession of which by him is a pertinent question at issue in a felony charge against him.[38]

In *Schmerber*, upholding *Breithaupt*, the U.S. Supreme Court opinion stated that the police could require a person arrested for a crime "to submit to fingerprinting, photographing, or measurements, to write or speak for identification, to appear in court, to stand, to assume a stance, to walk, or make a particular gesture"; furthermore, "we are told that the percentage of alcohol in the blood begins to diminish shortly after drinking stops, as the body functions to eliminate it from the system."[39] And in cases such as Schmerber's, there might be enough elimination of the alcohol in the blood system that to delay very long would not permit proving what the content was at the time of the accident. There

38. *Ibid.*, 291.
39. 384 U.S. 757, 764. On April 22, 1969, the U.S. Supreme Court reversed the conviction of John Davis from Meridian, Mississippi. He had been found guilty of rape. Because he had been among some 24 young Negroes rounded up in a "dragnet" arrest and brought to a station house and there fingerprinted, the Court said there was lack of probable cause to arrest and fingerprint him. His fingerprints were found by the FBI to match those at the scene of the crime. A new trial was ordered at which the fingerprints will not be admissible. *New York Times*, April 23, 1969, p. 18.

was no time to seek out a magistrate and secure a warrant. Those facts were enough for the majority of the Court to conclude "that the attempt to secure evidence of blood-alcohol content in this case was an appropriate incident to petitioner's arrest."[40] The conclusion left room for doubt. "That we hold today that the Constitution does not forbid the States minor intrusions into an individual's body under stringently limited conditions in no way indicates that it permits more substantial intrusions, or intrusions under other conditions."[41]

As in *Breithaupt*, there were strong dissents. Justice Douglas insisted they were dealing with a right of privacy which, since *Breithaupt*, "we have held to be within the penumbra of some specific guarantees of the Bill of Rights." He relied upon his own opinion in *Griswold* and concluded that "no clearer invasion of this right of privacy can be imagined than forcible blood-letting of the kind involved here."[42]

In his dissent, Justice Black showed his displeasure about the majority view that taking of blood was not testimony. He claimed that the

> compulsory extraction of petitioner's blood for analysis so that the person who analyzed it could give evidence to convict him had both a "testimonial" and a "communicative nature." The sole purpose . . . was to obtain "testimony" . . . to prove that petitioner had alcohol in his blood at the time he was arrested. And the purpose of the project was certainly "communicative" in that the analysis . . . was to supply information . . . to communicate to the court and jury that petitioner was more or less drunk.[43]

Again the Court was divided in finding a way to help society protect itself from the mischief of drunks and the right of anyone, drunk or not, to refuse to permit any use of his blood in order to convict him.

Taking blood and testing it under proper conditions is not an invasion of privacy, but can a person be forced to be given

40. 384 U.S., 770, 771.   41. *Ibid.*, 772.
42. *Ibid.*, 778, 779.   43. *Ibid.*, 774.

blood? That question was raised in the following two situations. They both involve matters of religious belief, but they more appropriately fit the category of cases included in this chapter.

Ceryl Linn Labrenz, an infant, eight days old, was suffering from an RH blood condition, and medical testimony indicated she would probably die if she were not given a blood transfusion.[44] Her parents had refused permission for the transfusion and also had indicated an unwillingness to take care of the child. It was claimed in Cook County Circuit Court that she had in effect been abandoned. A request was made that a guardian be appointed and authorized to consent to the transfusion. This was done, but in the trial a claim was made of an invasion of privacy.

One physician said that if the child lived without the transfusion her brain could be so injured that she would be mentally impaired for life. Another testified that the transfusion was not any more hazardous than the taking of an aspirin. But the parents nonetheless objected on grounds of religious belief, that the injection of another's blood into Ceryl's blood stream should not be permitted. In due course her condition improved, the guardianship was discharged, and she was released to her parents.

In the Illinois Supreme Court decision it was said, quoting from *Reynolds*:

> Laws are made for the government of actions, and while they cannot interfere with mere religious belief and opinions, they may with practices. Suppose one believed that human sacrifices were a necessary part of religious worship, would it be seriously contended that the civil government under which he lived could not interfere to prevent a sacrifice? Or if a wife religiously believed it was her duty to burn herself upon the funeral pyre of her dead husband, would it be beyond the power of the civil government to prevent her from carrying her belief into practice?[45]

44. *Wallace* v. *Labrenz*, 411 Ill. 618.
45. *Ibid.*, 625; *Reynolds* v. *U.S.*, 98 U.S., 166.

Then, referring to the more recent *Prince* case,[46] the opinion continued saying that the right to practice religion freely "does not include liberty to expose the community or the child to communicable disease or the latter to ill health or death." Parents might decide to become martyrs, but it did not follow they are free, in identical circumstances, to make martyrs of their children "before they have reached the age of full and legal discretion when they can make that choice for themselves."

A more recent case in Illinois involved a claim that an adult who did not wish to take blood to possibly save her life should not be forced to do so.[47] It was argued that First Amendment rights had been violated. Here an adult had refused blood transfusions to help her overcome the ill effects of peptic ulcers. Her attending physician stated during proceedings for the appointment of a "conservator" that when she denied the recommendation for the transfusions she was at the time "semi-disoriented" and not fully capable of understanding the circumstances. The conservator was duly appointed and consent obtained from him for the transfusions. Mrs. Brooks, the patient, her husband, and two adult children were admitted members of Jehovah's Witnesses. The opinion of the court stated that "so far as we have been advised or are aware, there is no reported decision in which this question has been squarely presented and recited."[48] But the opinion declared that where there was an adult member of a religious faith which claimed that blood transfusions were in violation of that faith and that the adult repeatedly and over a period of time refused the blood transfusions even with warning of the possible consequences, to require the transfusion was an unconstitutional infringement of her freedom. There was no minor child involved, only an adult. The First Amendment did protect the absolute right of every individual to freedom of religious beliefs and the exercise of those beliefs, subject only to the qualification that the exercise

46. *Prince* v. *Mass.*, 321 U.S. 158, 166, 167, 170 (1944).
47. *In re Estate of Brooks*, 32 Ill. 2d 361 (1965).
48. *Ibid.*, 372, 366.

may be limited by governmental action where the exercise endangers, clearly and presently, the public health, welfare, or morals.

> . . . when approaching death has so weakened the mental and physical faculties of a theretofore competent adult without minor children that she may properly be said to be incompetent, may she be judicially compelled to accept treatment of a nature which will probably preserve her life, but which is forbidden by her religious convictions, and which she has previously steadfastly refused to accept, knowing death would result from such refusal.[49]

The Court supported the view that there was an unconstitutional invasion of individual rights and referred to the compulsory vaccination and blood transfusion cases from other jurisdictions and the Illinios courts, but found them not the same. The compulsory vaccination cases were, went the opinion, "inapposite since society clearly can protect itself from the dangers of loathsome and contagious disease . . ." and it can protect itself from "polygamous marriage . . . because the practice consisted of overt acts determined to be deleterious to public morals and welfare."[50] To the Illinois Court there was no overt immoral activity on the part of Mrs. Brooks.

The Court had a problem, however, in relating the instant case to an earlier one in the District of Columbia.[51] There a federal judge ordered a blood transfusion to the mother of a minor child. He surmised that the state might well have an overriding interest in the welfare of the mother because, if she died, the child might become a ward of the state.

The Illinois Court concluded its decision about Mrs. Brooks:

> Even though we may consider appellant's beliefs unwise, foolish or ridiculous, in the absence of an overriding danger to society we may not permit interference therewith in the form of a conservatorship established in the

49. *Ibid.*, 365, 366.
50. *Ibid.*, 368.
51. *Application of President and Directors of Georgetown College, Inc.*, 331 F 2d 1000 (1964). Cert. denied.

waning hours of her life for the sole purpose of compelling her to accept medical treatment forbidden by her religious principles, and refused by her with full knowledge of the probable consequences.[52]

The next treatment of privacy situations begins with the now celebrated case of *Griswold* v. *Connecticut*.[53] It is unusual not only because of the broad support given the right of married couples to privacy but also because Justice Douglas used the majority opinion to develop his ideas of the high place he accords the right to privacy. It is of some further interest because of the concurring opinion of Justice Goldberg and the dissent by Justice Black.

In 1879, Connecticut enacted a law which made it a crime for anyone, including married people, to use contraceptives. This enactment came presumably as a result of a campaign to rid the state of sin and vice. The statute which Justice Stewart called an "uncommonly silly law" provided that any person who assists, abets, counsels, causes, hires, or commands another to use contraceptives may also be subject to prosecution.

During November, 1961, the executive director of the Planned Parenthood League of Connecticut, Mrs. Estelle Griswold, and Dr. Charles L. Buxton, a licensed physician, who served at the league's New Haven center as medical director, gave medical advice to married persons in violation of the statute. They were arrested, tried, and found guilty. The fine was $100 each. They appealed the conviction as a violation of the Fourteenth Amendment.

Justice Douglas reviewed the development of the extension of the Bill of Rights on a case-by-case basis after appeal to the U.S. Supreme Court. He indicated that the protections and guarantees of the Bill of Rights were also a part of the Fourteenth Amendment, putting all government in the United States under the same restraints. Consistent with the

52. 32 Ill. 2d, 373.

53. 381 U.S. 479 (1965). The *Michigan Law Review* 64, no. 2 (December 1965), is devoted to a "Symposium of the Griswold Case and the Right of Privacy."

First Amendment, he wrote, the state may not "contract the spectrum of available knowledge. The right of freedom of speech and press includes not only the right to utter or to print, but the right to distribute, the right to receive, the right to read, . . . and freedom of inquiry, freedom of thought, and freedom to teach. . . . Without those peripheral rights the specific rights would be less secure." [54]

Douglas then cited numerous cases involving freedom of association and privacy, the right of assembly—more than the mere right to attend a meeting—the right to express one's attitudes, and found them suggesting that the "specific guarantees in the Bill of Rights have penumbras, formed by emanations from those guarantees that help give them life and substance. . . . Various guarantees create zones of privacy." [55]

He then related the zones to the several amendments, and said that the Fourth affirmed "the right of the people to be secure in their persons, houses, papers, and effects against unreasonable searches and seizures." And the Fifth Amendment "enables the citizen to create a zone of privacy which government may not force him to surrender to his detriment." Citing *Boyd*, he said it gave "protection against all government invasions 'of the sanctity of a man's home and the privacies of life.' " He referred to *Mapp*, saying that the Fourth Amendment created a "right of privacy, no less important than any other right carefully and particularly reserved to the people." [56]

Without elaboration he also referred to the Ninth Amendment, and concluded: "We deal with a right of privacy older than the Bill of Rights—older than our political parties, older than our school system."

Justice Goldberg went beyond mere citation of the Ninth Amendment.

54. 381 U.S., 482, 483.
55. *Ibid.*, 483, 484.
56. *Ibid.*, 484, 485. See also, Luis Kutner, "The Neglected Ninth Amendment: The 'Other Rights' Retained by the People," *Marquette Law Review* 51, no. 2 (Fall 1967):121–142.

The language and history of the Ninth Amendment reveal that the Framers of the Constitution believed that there are additional fundamental rights, protected from governmental infringement which exist alongside those fundamental rights specifically mentioned in the first eight constitutional amendments. . . .

It was proffered to quiet expressed fears that a bill of specifically enumerated rights could not be sufficiently broad to cover all essential rights and that the specific mention of certain rights could be interpreted as a denial that others were protected.[57]

He said the Court had had little prior occasion to interpret the Ninth Amendment, but citing *Marbury* v. *Madison*, he said that it "cannot be presumed that any clause in the Constitution is intended to be without effect." He then had this to say:

The Ninth Amendment to the Constitution may be regarded by some as a recent discovery but since 1791 it has been a basic part of the Constitution which we are sworn to uphold. To hold that a right so basic and fundamental and so deep-rooted in our society as the right of privacy in marriage may be infringed because that right is not guaranteed in so many words by the first eight amendments to the Constitution is to ignore the Ninth Amendment and to give it no effect whatsoever.[58]

Justice Black, as indicated earlier, would not go along with such an all-embracing view. He not only would not accept the interpretation given the Ninth Amendment nonenumerated rights, but he did not like the emphasis given the right of privacy.

One of the most effective ways of diluting or expanding a constitutionally guaranteed right is to substitute for the crucial word or words of a constitutional guarantee another word or words, more or less flexible and more or less restricted in its meaning. This fact is well illustrated by the use of the term "right of privacy" as a comprehen-

57. 381 U.S., 488, 489.
58. 1 Cr. 137, 174 (1802); *Griswold* v. *Conn.*, 491.

sive substitute for the Fourth Amendment's guarantee against "unreasonable searches and seizures".... I get nowhere in this case by talk about a constitutional "right of privacy" as an emanation from one or more constitutional provisions.[59]

The introduction of the Ninth Amendment as a source of support was also put aside by Black.

Moreover, one would certainly have to look far beyond the language of the Ninth Amendment to find that the framers vested in this Court any such awesome veto powers over lawmaking, either by the States or by the Congress. Nor does anything in the history of the Amendment offer any support for such a shocking doctrine.... I cannot rely on the Due Process Clause or the Ninth Amendment or any mysterious and uncertain natural law concept as a reason for striking down this state law.[60]

Whether the majority view in *Griswold* is notice that government cannot control private acts of individuals if they do not directly harm society remains to be seen. But it is doubtful that all private acts are to be sanctioned merely because not very many people know about them.[61]

Loving v. *Virginia* was decided in 1967.[62] It invalidated state miscegenation statutes. As late as the early 1950's, nearly two-thirds of the states had laws prohibiting the marriage of persons of different races. The situation prior to *Loving* can be illustrated by some selected cases.

59. *Griswold* v. *Conn.*, 509, 510.
60. *Ibid.*, 519, 522.
61. For a comparison between English law and practice and that of the U.S., see Hart, *Law, Liberty and Morality*, p. 82. He argues that it is pointless to make a distinction between acts in private which are condoned because they are not known or are not offensive to the public—being private—and the act itself. If condemned because it is immoral, then it would be punishable wherever committed (p. 45). He insists that there is no evidence that society can be preserved only through the enforcement of morality "as such."
62. 388 U.S. 1.

An early Georgia case involved the marriage of a white
man and a black woman.[63] They were prosecuted for violating a state statute prohibiting such marriages. In the U.S.
Circuit Court for the Southern District of Georgia, the Court
said it

> will not discuss the argument of defendant's counsel to
> the effect that the intermarriages of whites and blacks
> do not constitute an evil or injury against which the state
> should protect itself. . . . It is enough, for the purpose of
> its duty, for the court to ascertain that by a legitimate
> and settled policy the state of Georgia has declared such
> marriages unlawful and void.[64]

A claim was made that the statute was violative of the defendant's equal protection of the laws guaranteed by the Fourteenth Amendment, but to no avail.

The earliest mention of the power of the states to regulate
marriages was a brief comment by the U.S. Supreme Court
in *Plessy* v. *Ferguson*. "Laws forbidding the intermarriage of the
two races may be said in a technical sense to interfere with
the freedom of contract, and yet have been universally
recognized as within the police power of the State."[65]

The trial judge in the lower court in *Loving* best expressed
the generally accepted view supporting miscegenation statutes.

> Almighty God created the races white, black, yellow,
> malay and red and he placed them on separated conti-
> nents. And but for the interference with his arrangement
> there would be no cause for such marriages. The fact
> that he separated the races shows that he did not intend
> for the races to mix.[66]

63. *State* v. *Tutty*, 41 F. 753 (1890).
64. *Ibid.*, 762.
65. 163 U.S. 537, 545 (1896). Apparently the first U.S. Supreme
Court decision referring to the power of a state to regulate marriage
was *Plessy*, but the case of *Maynard* v. *Hill*, 125 U.S. 190 (1888),
involved the Washington *Territory*. By the Act of 1836, the Congress
had granted the Territory power "to all rightful subjects of legislation." Said the Court, "Marriage, . . . has always been subject to
the control of the legislature" (204, 205).
66. 388 U.S. 1, 3.

Chief Justice Warren delivered the opinion of the U.S. Supreme Court in *Loving*. The issue, he stated, was whether the Virginia statute prohibiting marriages solely on the basis of racial classifications violates the Equal Protection and Due Process Clauses of the Fourteenth Amendment. The opinion held that they were violated by the statute.

In 1958, two Virginia residents, Mildred Jeter, a black woman, and Richard Loving, a white man, were married in the District of Columbia pursuant to its laws. Shortly thereafter they returned to Virginia. They were later indicted and sentenced to one year in jail, but this was suspended on condition they leave the state for twenty-five years! The convictions were approved in the Virginia Court of Appeals.

Warren observed that at the time sixteen states had interracial bans, but that during the prior fifteen years some fourteen states had repealed them. He also noted that the instant case presented a constitutional question never before addressed to the Court. But the opinion was relatively brief.

> There is patently no legitimate overriding purpose independent of invidious racial discrimination which justifies this classification. The fact that Virginia prohibits only interracial marriages involving white persons demonstrates that the racial classifications must stand on their own justification, as measures designed to maintain White Supremacy. We have consistently denied the constitutionality of measures which restrict the rights of citizens on account of race. There can be no doubt that restricting the freedom to marry solely because of racial classifications violates the central meaning of the Equal Protection Clause.[67]

To prevent hasty marriages many states have enacted laws requiring a waiting period of from one to five days from the time a marriage license was applied for until it was actually valid for use. Some of them permit a waiver of the waiting period which may help sustain their validity.

A related state requirement has been to require premarital and prenatal examinations. Their use, obviously, is intended

67. *Ibid.*, 11, 12.

to try to stamp out venereal disease and to protect the partners and their offspring. The leading case upholding such rules is *Peterson* v. *Widule*, in which the Court said "society has a right to protect itself from extinction and its members from a fate worse than death."[68]

The police power follows the scientific trail in the field of public health. Long ago the U.S. Supreme Court upheld the power of the states to enact laws which would require vaccinations. In a Massachusetts case in 1905 the Court inquired whether any right "given, or secured by the Constitution is invaded by the statute."[69] The statute authorized local health boards, under certain conditions, to require the vaccination of all inhabitants of the city or town, except to children who presented medical certificates that they should not be vaccinated. Jacobson objected to the vaccination claiming it was both useless and dangerous. To him the requirement was

> unreasonable, arbitrary, and oppressive, and therefore, hostile to the inherent right of every free man to care for his own body and health in such a way as to him seems best; and that the execution of such a law against one who objects to vaccination, no matter for what reason, is nothing short of an assault upon his person.[70]

This line of reasoning was not supported by the Court. It found that there

> are manifold restraints to which every person is necessarily subject to the common good. On any other basis organized society could not exist with safety to its members. . . . Real liberty for all could not exist under the operation of a principle which recognizes the right of each individual person to use his own, whether in respect of his person or his property, regardless of the injury that may be done to others.[71]

To require vaccination was a clear legislative right intended

68. 157 Wis. 641, 647 (1914).
69. *Jacobson* v. *Mass.*, 197 U.S. 11, 25.
70. *Ibid.*, 26.
71. *Ibid.*

to secure "the general comfort, health, and prosperity of the state."[72]

The door was left open to the right of the individual to dispute governmental authority when it interfered with the supremacy of the individual will, but

> it is equally true that in every well-ordered society charged with the duty of conserving the safety of its members the rights of the individual in respect to his liberty may at times, under the pressure of great dangers, be subjected to such restraint, to be enforced by reasonable regulations, as the safety of the general public may demand.[73]

Compulsory X-rays do not violate any claim of the invasion of personal privacy. In a Washington case[74] in 1952 all students registering at the University of Washington were required to have a chest X-ray for the purpose of discovering possible tubercular infections. Although Miss Holcomb objected on religious grounds, the facts more nearly fit the purposes of this chapter than elsewhere. The Washington Supreme Court said that the regulation did not violate any constitutional protection. The rule for the X-rays was a means of protecting the public interest. That interest which was threatened was the health of "all students and employees of the University. It may lawfully be protected."[75]

The dissent by Justice Hamley is worth noting.

> Attendance at the University of Washington is not compulsory. I am therefore inclined to believe that the board of regents was not exercising the police power of the state in promulgating the regulation in question. It was simply the exercise of administrative power such as is vested in all public officers with respect to the use and occupancy of public property and the performance of official duties. If this be true, then the constitutional guarantees respecting the free exercise of religion are not

72. *Ibid.*
73. *Ibid.*, 29.
74. *State ex rel Holcomb* v. *Armstrong*, 39 Wash. 2d 860.
75. *Ibid.*, 864.

directly involved. They are drawn into issue only where there is an element of compulsion.[76]

"Three generations of imbeciles are enough." So wrote Justice Holmes in *Buck* v. *Bell*.[77] He was supporting a Virginia statute authorizing sterilization of mental defectives. The superintendent of the State Colony for Epileptics and Feeble Minded was ordered to perform the operation of salpingectomy upon Carrie Buck. Carrie was committed to the state colony as a feeble-minded person. According to the facts, she was the daughter of a feeble-minded mother in the same institution, and the mother of an illegitimate feeble-minded child.

A 1924 act of Virginia provided that under certain conditions the health of a patient and the welfare of society could be promoted by the sterilization of mental defectives, and it could be done without serious pain or substantial danger to life.

Arguments before the Court indicated that many defective persons if discharged from the colony could be a menace, but if incapable of procreating might be discharged with safety and become self-supporting with benefit to themselves and society. The Court agreed that there was support for the position that "heredity plays an important part in the transmission of insanity, imbecility, etc."[78] Justice Holmes found no difficulty in depriving individuals like Carrie Buck of any rights of motherhood.

> We have seen more than once that public welfare may call upon the best citizens for their lives. It would be strange if it could not call upon those who already sap the strength of the State for these lesser sacrifices, often not felt to be such by those concerned, in order to prevent our being swamped with incompetence. It is better for all the world, if instead of waiting to execute degenerate offspring for crime, or to let them starve for their imbecility, society can prevent those who are manifestly unfit from continuing their kind.[79]

Oklahoma gave the welfare of society a different twist in the 1935 Habitual Criminal Act. It sought to prevent the

76. *Ibid.*, 867.   77. 274 U.S. 200, 207 (1927).
78. *Ibid.*, 206.   79. *Ibid.*, 207.

state from having to execute degenerate offspring of habitual criminals through sterilization of the would-be father.

The statute defined an habitual criminal as one who had been convicted two or more times for crimes amounting to felonies, involving moral turpitude, and who was sentenced to terms of imprisonment. If a person was so sentenced, proceedings should be entered to render him sexually sterile.

The U.S. Supreme Court in *Skinner* v. *Oklahoma*[80] viewed the statute with less than enthusiasm. Skinner had a habit of stealing and robbing and getting caught and sentenced. This happened three times, and an order directed him sterilized. The Supreme Court of Oklahoma affirmed the order.

Skinner, appropriately distressed, objected to the constitutionality of the statute as penal in character, contending that sterilization would be a cruel and unusual punishment and would violate the Fourteenth Amendment. The U.S. Supreme Court passed those objections aside saying there was one feature which clearly condemned it. "That is, its failure to meet the requirements of the equal protection clause of the Fourteenth Amendment." The Court noted that those who committed grand larceny three times could be sterilized, but those who were habitual embezzlers would not be so subjected. "Oklahoma makes no attempt to say that he who commits larceny by trespass or trick or fraud has biologically inheritable traits which he who commits embezzlement lacks."[81]

Justice Douglas, giving the opinion for the Court, expressed concern about Arthur Skinner's rights. "When the law lays an unequal hand on those who have committed intrinsically the same quality of offense and sterilizes one and not the other, it has made as invidious a discrimination as if it had selected a particular race or nationality for oppressive treatment."[82]

Buck v. *Bell* was not overruled, but Douglas had this to say about basic rights.

We are dealing here with legislation which involves one of the basic civil rights of man. Marriage and procreation

80. 316 U.S. 535 (1942).
81. *Ibid.*, 538, 541.
82. *Ibid.*, 541.

are fundamental to the very existence and survival of the race. The power to sterilize, if exercised, may have subtle, far reaching and devastating effects. In evil or reckless hands can cause races or types which are inimical to the dominant group to wither and disappear. There is no redemption for the individual whom the law touches. . . . He is forever deprived of a basic liberty.[83]

As has been observed, the privileges of the First Amendment provide a preferred status or superior position of rights, but some claimed religious practices, unlike plural marriages, do not overcome the power of the state to regulate some of them in the name of public safety.

A Kentucky[84] and a Tennessee[85] case illustrate this. The Kentucky legislature enacted a statute which would punish those who displayed and handled snakes in connection with religious services or meetings. The statute was attacked as being beyond the legitimate exercise of the police power because, it was claimed, many species of snakes are harmless and their handling and exhibition are "unattended by danger." But the Supreme Court of Kentucky would not agree. The Court observed that it is true that many snakes are not poisonous, but many are. The religious performances under question were not done by a zoologist, a herpetologist, and only they or an experienced woodsman would be able to distinguish a poisonous from a nonpoisonous snake. Since that was the case the legislature had the right to forbid the practice altogether. The public was entitled to protection. "The peace and safety of the state involve the protection of the lives and health of its children, as well as the obedience to its laws."[86]

The Tennessee case is similar. Tom Harden was convicted for violating a statute prohibiting anyone from handling snakes in such a manner as would endanger the life or health of any person. He was a member of the Holiness Church. A part of

83. *Ibid.*
84. *Lawson* v. *Commonwealth*, 291 Ky. 437 (1942).
85. *Harden* v. *State*, 188 Tenn. 17 (1948).
86. 291 Ky. 437, 446, citing *People* v. *Pierson*, 176 N.Y. 201.

the ritual, it seemed, was to handle poisonous snakes and entwine them around their necks and bodies to test the proof of their sincerity and beliefs. The court concluded that the practice was dangerous to the life and health of the people and the practice could be forbidden by the legislature.

Recent concerns about the use of drugs is illustrated by the recent case of *U.S.* v. *Kuch.*[87] It also involved the right to the free exercise of religion.

Judith H. Kuch was indicted for unlawfully obtaining and transferring marijuana and for the unlawful sale, delivery, and possession of LSD. She claimed she was an ordained minister of the "Neo-American Church," and the provisions of the U.S. Code she was claimed to have violated were an infringement of her constitutional right. According to the opinion, she presented no subjective evidence as to her individual beliefs but chose to rely on her office in the church and proof as so the requirements of the church as constituted. In order to join the church a member had to subscribe as follows:

> The psychedelic substances, such as LSD, are the true Host of the Church, not drugs. They are sacramental foods, manipulations of the Grace of God, of the infinite imagination of the Self, and therefore belong to everyone; . . . We do not encourage the ingestion of psychedelics by those who are unprepared.[88]

According to the testimony, the church specifies that "it is the Religious *duty* of all members to partake of the sacraments on regular occasions."[89] Some of the literature on the church asserted that the members "have the *right* to practice our religion, even if we are a bunch of filthy, drunken bums."[90]

The decision would not sustain the claim.

> Defendant misconceives the Constitution and the decisions when she claims in effect an unbridled right to practice her beliefs. The public interest is paramount and if properly determined the Congress may inhibit or

87. 288 F.S. 439 (1968).
88. *Ibid.*, 443.
89. *Ibid.*
90. *Ibid.*

prevent acts as opposed to beliefs even where those acts are in accord with religious convictions or beliefs. If individual religious conviction permits one to act contrary to civic duty, public health and the criminal laws of the land, then the right to be let alone in one's belief with all the spiritual peace it guarantees would be destroyed in the resulting breakdown of society. There is abroad among some in the land today a view that the individual is free to do anything he wishes.[91]

The judge complained that the U.S. Supreme Court had given little guidance in what is and what is not religion. "Indeed, the Court appears to have avoided the problem with studied frequency in recent years."[92] But he found that the statutes at issue had a rational and constitutional basis and were enacted to preserve public safety, health, and order, and would be enforced.

In the interest of promoting public health and safety, legislatures and city councils have enacted statutes and ordinances designed to enforce standards. Their enforcement raises questions about privacy and some recent U.S. Supreme Court cases illustrate the point.

A Baltimore health inspector was seeking the source of rat infestation in a residential area.[93] After receiving no response from a knock on Frank's door, he looked around the immediate area and observed an accumulation of trash and debris and some rodent feces. Frank's house appeared to be in an extreme state of decay. While inspecting the area, Frank appeared and asked the inspector to explain his presence. The inspector explained he had evidence of rodent infestation and asked for permission to inspect the basement area of Frank's home. Frank refused. The next afternoon in the company of police officers, the inspector returned, but he received no response from a knock on the door. In company of the police officers, the inspector again examined the accumulation in the rear

91. *Ibid.*, 445.

92. *Ibid.*, 443. But it was all right for members of the Native American Church, American Indians, to use "peyote," for they had a long history of its use. *People* v. *Woody*, 61 Cal. 2d 716 (1964).

93. *Frank* v. *Maryland*, 359 U.S. 360 (1959).

yard and then obtained a warrant for Frank's arrest. It was alleged that there was a violation of the city code intended to promote the public health.

The courts upheld Frank's conviction. In the U.S. Supreme Court, Justice Frankfurter reviewed the history of the constitutional protection against official invasion of the citizen's home and reason for the development of the right to remain free from ransacking homes via the general warrant. From this development he found two protections had emerged.

> The first . . . is the right to be secure from intrusion of personal privacy, the right to shut the door on officials of the state unless the entry is under proper authority of law. The second . . . is self-preservation: the right to resist unauthorized entry which has as its design the securing of information to fortify the coercive power of the state . . . which may be used to effect a further deprivation of life or liberty or property.[94]

But Frankfurter would not invoke those protections in behalf of Frank. He found nothing in the situation which sought information or evidence for a criminal prosecution. All the City of Baltimore wished to do was to maintain some minimum community standards for the well-being of the people. The liberty "that is asserted is the absolute right to refuse the consent for an inspection designed and pursued solely for protection for community's health, even when the inspection is conducted with due regard for every convenience of time and place."[95]

Four justices dissented. They all felt that about the only people left with a right to privacy were suspected criminals. Justice Douglas wrote:

> "The security of one's privacy against arbitrary intrusion is at the core of the Fourth Amendment—is basic to a free society." Now that resounding phrase is watered down to embrace only certain invasions of one's privacy. If officials come to inspect for sanitary conditions, they might come with warrant and demand entry as a right. . . . In some

94. *Ibid.*, 365.
95. *Ibid.*, 366.

States, the health inspectors are none other than the
police themselves. In some States the presence of unsanitary conditions give rise to criminal prosecutions. . . . The
right is the guarantee against invasion of the home by
officers without a warrant. No officer of government is
authorized to penalize the citizen because he invokes his
constitutional protection.[96]

The next cases considered concern invasions of homes and
of search, but the methods employed are unusual.

In March, 1956, Mrs. Phipps applied for welfare payments
for herself and her nine minor children.[97] She disclosed that
her husband was employed and living at home. She was
denied aid. In October the same year she again applied for
aid and stated that since her prior filing she had sought
divorce from her husband and he was living away from
the family. Welfare payments began and continued until the
end of January, 1959. From investigation or informers the
Welfare Department learned that Mr. Phipps was still living
at home and the marriage was not actually disrupted.

Between 2:00 and 3:00 A.M. on January 28, 1959, Welfare
Department workers went to the Phipps home to investigate
the truth of the reports that Mr. Phipps continued to live at
home. During the trial it was stated that the visit was made at
that unusual hour to preclude an anticipated explanation, if
Mr. Phipps was there, that he was merely visiting the children.
As investigators approached the home, Mr. Phipps was
leaving by the back door. Mrs. Phipps and several of the
children were inside. Both the senior Phippses were fully
dressed. Mrs. Phipps stated that Mr. Phipps was there during
the evening and was still there awaiting the return of a teenage
daughter who had gone to attend a dance. They admitted
he visited the home from time to time, but when he remained
overnight he slept in a panel truck in the back yard. The
California court said they were satisfied that the evidence was
sufficient to support the finding that Mrs. Phipps had made
false representations with the intent to defraud and she had

96. *Ibid.*, 375, citing *Wolf* v. *Colo.*, 338 U.S. 25, 27.
97. *People* v. *Phipps*, 191 Cal. App. 2d 448 (1961).

no intention of keeping a promise to report the return of her husband if that event occurred.

Similar circumstances prevailed in the Parrish case six years later, but the outcome was different.[98] On November 21, 1962, the Board of Supervisors of Alameda County ordered the county welfare director to institute a series of unannounced early morning searches of homes of the county's welfare recipients for the purpose of detecting the presence of unauthorized males. The searches were called "operation week end." Members of the staff of the Welfare Department did not seek nor have search warrants. It developed that the workers who conducted the search were not to restrict the searches to homes of those whom they had probable cause to suspect. Indeed, a majority of the homes to be visited were those under no suspicion at all, but this was by design to show the efficiency of the welfare program and the low incidence of fraud.

These early morning visits began after 6:30 A.M. on Sunday, January 13, 1963. The workers arrived at homes in pairs, one going to the back door, the other to the front. They would knock and ask to be admitted. The occupant would be told the identity of the visitors, and the search would begin over the entire dwelling with special attention given to beds, closets, bathrooms, and other possible places of concealment.

The California court found the searches invalid. It observed that the county authorities conceded it sought no warrants and that it lacked probable cause for arresting anyone. The county defense was that they had not forcibly entered any home. The searches took place with consent freely and voluntarily given.

But the court observed that the methods employed by the welfare workers were much more than a mere request for admission.

> Thus we need not determine here whether a request for entry, voiced by one in a position of authority under circumstances which suggest that some official reprisal attained a refusal, is itself sufficient to vitiate an affir-

98. *Parrish* v. *Civil Service Commission*, 425 P 2d 223 (1967).

mative response by an individual who had not been ap-
prised of his Fourth Amendment rights. The persons
subjected to the instant operation confronted far more
than amorphous threat of official displeasure which necessarily attends any such request. The request for entry by
persons whom the beneficiaries knew possessed virtually
unlimited power over their very livelihood posed a threat
which was far more certain, immediate, and substantial.[99]

Even if the welfare recipient had been advised of his rights,
the California court would have none of it. The operation
was based on the assumption that the welfare agency could
withhold aid if the worker was denied entry and permission to
search. They would threaten to stop payments to any who
insisted upon his rights to privacy. The official demand was
enough to make any consent involuntary and coercive.

The opinion concluded, noting that the Welfare Department had to be concerned with "ferreting out fraud in the
inexcusable garnering of welfare payments not truly deser-
ved. . . . It is surely not beyond the competence of the department to conduct appropriate investigations without violence
to human dignity and within the confines of the Constitution."[100] No more need be said.

Another welfare case shows that health standards can be
enforced. A New York case is in point.[101] David Wilkie, a
recipient of old-age assistance, was denied continued payments
because he refused to move from his place of residence to
better quarters. His residence was under a barn in a nest of
rags. Welfare Commissioner O'Connor was willing to increase
Wilkie's monthly payments to offset the higher living costs
in a place which would provide a civilized standard of living.
Wilkie insisted he had a right to live as he pleased. The
opinion of the New York court stated that "one would admire
his independence if he were not so dependent, but he had no
right to defy the standards and conventions of civilized society
while being supported at public expense."[102]

99. *Ibid.*, 229.
100. *Ibid.*, 234.
101. *Wilkie* v. *O'Connor*, 25 N.Y. Supp. 2d 617 (1941).
102. *Ibid.*, 619.

Even though Wilkie claimed that he had not suffered physically by his mode of living, the court was not impressed. "After all he should not demand that the public, at its expense, allow him to experiment with the manner of living which is likely to endanger his health so that he will become a still greater expense to the public." [103]

Frank v. *Maryland* was decided in 1959 and, as indicated above, involved inspections by health officials. Eight years later it was overruled. In *Camera* v. *Municipal Court of the City and County of San Francisco*,[104] Camera was charged with violating the Housing Code. He claimed it invalid.

On November 6, 1963, an inspector of the Department of Health went to an apartment building to make a routine inspection for possible violations of the Code. The Code provided that apartment house operators pay an annual license fee to defray the costs of the inspections. Camera refused to permit the inspectors entry because he did not find that they had a search warrant. Two days later a return visit was made, again without a warrant, and again, entry was refused. A citation was then mailed to Camera ordering him to appear at the office of the district attorney. He failed to appear. He was arrested and released on bail.

Camera argued that the Fourth and Fourteenth Amendments should deny entry into his premises without a warrant and also without probable cause to believe a violation actually existed. The lower court sustained the Code relying on the decision in *Frank* and related cases. But the U.S. Supreme Court took a contrary view and to the extent that the decision in *Frank* sanctioned warrantless inspection, it was overruled.

Justice White delivered the opinion of the Court.

We may agree that a routine inspection of the physical condition of private property is a less hostile intrusion than the typical policeman's search for the fruits and instrumentalities of crime. For this reason alone, *Frank* differed from the great bulk of Fourth Amendment cases

103. *Ibid.*
104. 387 U.S. 523 (1967).

which have been considered by this Court. But we cannot agree that the Fourth Amendment interests at stake in these inspection cases are merely "peripheral." It is surely anomalous to say that the individual and his private property are fully protected only when the individual is suspected of criminal behavior. For instance, even the most law-abiding citizen has a very tangible interest in limiting the circumstances under which the sanctity of his home may be broken by official authority, for the possibility of criminal entry under the guise of official sanction is a serious threat to personal and family security.[105]

White found that laws for the regulation of standards concerning health, housing, fire, and the like are enforced by criminal processes. And refusal here to permit an inspection was itself a crime. Referring to *Frank*, he said that it would permit "rubber stamp" warrants which did not give the property owner much protection, and he would not accept the practice.

In our opinion, these arguments unduly discount the purposes behind the warrant machinery contemplated by the Fourth Amendment. Under the present system, when the inspector demands entry, the occupant had no way of knowing whether enforcement of the municipal code involved requires inspection of his premises, no way of knowing the lawful limit of the inspector's power to search, and no way of knowing whether the inspector himself is acting under proper authorization.[106]

The City and County urged approval of the warrantless procedure, saying the public interest demanded it. The health and safety, it was urged, is dependent upon minimum fire, housing, and sanitation codes and the only way to get compliance was by a routine inspection everywhere. This, too, was unacceptable to White.

But we think this argument misses the mark. The question is not, at this stage at least, whether these inspections may be made, but whether they may be made without

105. *Ibid.*, 530, 531.
106. *Ibid.*, 532.

a warrant. . . . In summary, we hold that administrative searches of the kind at issue here are significant intrusions upon the interests protected.[107]

At that point, *Frank* v. *Maryland* lost its punch.

The warrant procedure is designed to guarantee that a decision to search private property is justified by a reasonable governmental interest. But reasonableness is still the ultimate standard. If a valid public interest justifies the intrusion contemplated, then there is probable cause to issue a suitably restricted search warrant.[108]

Another inspection case decided that same year involved an effort of a fire inspector to inspect a commercial warehouse. There was no warrant and admission was refused. Of special interest is the dissent by Justice Clark.

I ask: why go through such a pretense? . . . Why the ceremony, the delay, the expense, the abuse of the search warrant. In my view this will not only destroy its integrity but will degrade the magistrate issuing the warrant and soon bring disrepute not only upon the practice but upon the judicial process. It will be very costly to the city and paper work incident to the issuance of the proper warrants, and loss of time of inspectors and waste of time of magistrates and result in more annoyance to the public. It will also be more burdensome to the occupant of the premises to be inspected. Under a search warrant the inspector can enter any time he chooses. Under the existing procedure he can enter only at reasonable times and invariably the convenience of the occupant is considered.[109]

The Court majority insisted upon warrants.

Legislators and judges have not always been mindful of the urging of John Stuart Mill who, a century ago, published his famous *On Liberty*. In one of the strongest defenses of freedom ever written he said:

107. *Ibid.*, 533, 534.
108. *Ibid.*, 539.
109. *See* v. *City of Seattle*, 387 U.S. 541, 554, 555 (1967).

That the only purpose for which power can rightfully be exercised over any member of a civilized community, against his will, is to prevent harm to others. His own good, either physical or moral, is not a sufficient warrant. He cannot rightfully be compelled to do or forbear because it will be better for him to do so, because it will make him happier, because, in the opinion of others, to do would be wise, or even right.[110]

110. R. B. McCallum edition (Oxford: B. Blackwell, 1947), pp. 8, 9.

V

Future Directions

———◆———

Forty years ago Justice Brandeis suggested the direction which law enforcement officers should take in carrying out their assigned duties. He thought there were some rules of conduct they should observe.

> Our government is the potent, the omnipresent, teacher. For good or ill, it teaches the whole people by example. Crime is contagious. If the Government becomes a law-breaker, it breeds contempt for law; it invites every man to become a law unto himself; it invites anarchy. To declare that in the administration of the criminal law the end justifies the means—to declare that the government may commit crimes in order to secure the conviction of a private criminal—would bring terrible retribution. Against that pernicious doctrine this Court should resolutely set its face.[1]

During the intervening years there has been growing concern that judges have made law enforcement more difficult and, according to some, nearly impossible. To Justice Black, the Bill of Rights means what it says, and of course the rights protected by the Bill make it difficult to convict those accused of crime. It was intended that the accused be protected as innocent until proven guilty.

The results of many of the opinions of the justices of the U.S. Supreme Court which have been presented in the

1. *Olmstead* v. *U.S.*, 277 U.S. 485 (1928).

foregoing chapters undoubtedly were in the minds of many of those who opposed the nomination of Justice Fortas as chief justice in 1968.[2] Many felt then and continue to believe that the trend of judicial pronouncements has been to favor the ones who engage in crime and do not really affect the innocent who may get into the clutches of the law. Those who accept that view appear to believe that society will not be safe again—or as safe as it once was—until the rules are changed.

One view has been forcibly stated by Frank J. McGarr, former First Assistant Attorney for the Northern District of Illinois and a member of the law faculty of Loyola University in Chicago. At a 1960 conference at the Northwestern University School of Law he had this to say:

> I think we are living in an era where in the course of emphasis upon individual civil liberties the Court has come dangerously close to upsetting the balance which it is necessary to preserve between the rights of the individual and the rights of society as a whole. In tying the hands of our law enforcement agencies under the philosophy that a criminal prosecution is sort of a sporting contest where the odds must be even, we may be submitting our society to the inroads of a criminal element which ultimately we will not be able to control. I am not suggesting as a blood-thirsty prosecutor that everybody is guilty and they should be marched to jail without a trial. But, I do suggest to you that we consider how far we have strayed from the proposition that the function of a trial is to send a guilty man to jail and acquit an innocent man. If we disturb that function or envision the function of a trial to be anything else, we are stripping the government of the power to protect us against criminals and crime.[3]

During his 1968 campaign, President Nixon was critical of what have been termed extensions of criminal defendants' rights by the courts, especially the U.S. Supreme Court.

2. See especially the *Congressional Record* for May 22, 1968, S 6095–6113, and May 23, 1968, S 6201–6246.

3. "The Exclusionary Rule: An Ill Conceived and Ineffective Remedy," in Claude R. Sowle, ed., *Police Power and Individual Freedom* (Chicago: Aldine Pub. Co., 1962), p. 103.

The *Congressional Record* for May 23, 1968, reports his position paper which in effect was an endorsement of Title III of the omnibus crime bill then in its final stages for passage.

> Organized crime is a secret society. By denying to State and Federal law enforcement agencies the tools to penetrate that secrecy, the President and the Attorney General are unwittingly guaranteeing the leaders of organized crime a privileged sanctuary from which to proceed with the systematic corruption of American life.[4]

His views on court decisions went thus: "Let us always respect, as I do, our courts and those who serve them, but let us also recognize that some of our courts in their decisions have gone too far in weakening the peace forces as against the criminal forces in this country."[5]

These were obvious and direct references to the decisions of the U.S. Supreme Court. Whether needed to influence the passage of the 1968 crime bill cannot be determined, but the statements were issued on the eve of its passage—a bill intended to put strong restraints on the Court's interpretation of the rights of defendants. One hopes that those in the Congress supporting the most restrictive features of the bill, especially Titles II and III, had the rights of the ordinary man in mind as much as they did in their proper desire to ferret out the evil ones to whom the strong restraints were being directed. Even so, the words of Justice Douglas in *Osborn* may haunt them in the years ahead.

> The citizen is completely unaware of the invasion of his privacy. The invasion of privacy is not limited to him, but extends to his friends and acquaintances—to everyone who happens to talk on the telephone with the suspect or who happens to come within the range of the electronic device. Their words are also intercepted; their privacy is also shattered. . . .
> Such practice can only have a damaging effect on our society. Once sanctioned, there is every indication that

4. *Congressional Record*, May 23, 1968, S 6242.
5. Congressional Quarterly, *Guide to Current American Government* (Fall 1968), p. 18.

their use will indiscriminately spread. The time may come when no one can be sure whether his words are being recorded for use at some future time; when everyone will fear that his most secret thoughts are no longer his own, but belong to the government; when the most confidential and intimate conversations are always open to eager, prying ears. When that time comes, privacy, and with it liberty, will be gone.[6]

United States Circuit Judge Henry J. Friendly, mentioned as a possible Nixon appointee to the Court, was reported late in 1968 as contending that the U.S. Supreme Court had expanded the privilege against self-incrimination far beyond its intended scope and that it seriously impedes the state in the basic task of providing for the security of the individual and his property. Lecturing at the University of Cincinnati College of Law, he said that the time had come when the nation needed to face up to the difficult task of considering an amendment to the self-incrimination clause that would preserve all that the framers said and "some" of the Supreme Court's "extensions," but which would modify others, eliminate some altogether, and provide safeguards against accretions which were probably in "the making." He accused the Court of treating the self-incrimination clause with almost "religious adulation."[7]

Judge Friendly was especially critical of decisions relating to the defendant's right to counsel and the *Miranda* decision of 1966.[8] To straighten out the U.S. Supreme Court he proposed a lengthy amendment to the U.S. Constitution. The proposed amendment is as follows:

The clause of the fifth amendment to the Constitution of the United States, "nor shall be compelled in any criminal case to be a witness against himself," shall not be construed to prohibit:

(1) Interrogating any person or requesting him to

6. *Osborn* v. *U.S.*, 385 U.S., 353, 354 (1966).
7. *Lincoln Journal Star*, November 10, 1968, p. 2 EE.
8. *Miranda* v. *Arizona*, 384 U.S. 436. The case concerned the admissibility of confessions.

furnish goods or chattels, including books, papers and other writings, without warning that he is not obliged to comply, unless such person has been taken into custody because of, or has been charged with, a crime to which the interrogation or request relates.

(2) Comment by the judge at any criminal trial on previous refusal by the defendant to answer inquiries relevant to the crime before a grand jury or similar investigating body, or before a judicial officer charged with the duty of presiding over his interrogation, provided that he shall have been afforded the assistance of counsel when being so questioned and shall have then been warned that he need not answer; that if he does answer, his answer may be used against him in court; and that if he does not answer, the judge may comment on his refusal.

(3) Compulsory production, in response to reasonable subpoena or similar process, of any goods or chattels, including books, papers and other writings.

(4) Dismissal, suspension or other discipline of any officer or employee of the United States, a state, or any agency or subdivision thereof, or any person licensed by any of them, for refusal, after warning of the consequences, to answer a relevant question concerning his official or professional conduct in an investigation relating thereto, or the introduction in evidence of any answer given to any such question, provided that such person shall have been afforded the assistance of counsel.

(5) Requiring a person lawfully arrested for or charged with crime to identify himself and make himself available for visual and auditory investigation and for reasonable scientific and medical tests, provided the assistance of counsel has been afforded except when urgency otherwise requires.

(6) Requiring registration or reporting reasonably necessary for a proper governmental purpose, provided that no registration or report so compelled shall be admissible as evidence of any crime revealed therein.

Judge Friendly did not consider his proposals as interdependent. And presumably because of ready conflict with the First Amendment, he offered another: "Nothing in the foregoing shall apply to interrogation, registration, reporting, or the production of writings with respect to religious, political or social beliefs or associations."[9]

He insisted that his proposals were not designed to repeal "everything" the Court had done on the subject, but "if our only choices were repeal or what we now have, I would unhesitatingly choose the latter."

These proposals or some similar may well be the subject of debate in the 91st Congress and thereafter unless President Nixon is able to appoint a sufficient number of "strict constructionists" to the Court before any such amendment proceeded far in the amending process.

Whatever one's position on the "law and order" issue of the 1968 campaign or his concern about judicial pronouncements toward leniency, the words of Justice Holmes in *Olmstead* cannot be forgotten: ". . . and for my part I think it is a less evil that some criminals should escape than that the Government should play an ignoble part."[10]

To some it may loom that the end of the Warren Court will mean the end and even the possible reversal of "liberal" decisions in recent years which have clarified—on a case-by-case basis—portions of the Bill of Rights and the Fourteenth Amendment. But *stare decisis* is very controlling to the doctrinaire strict constructionist, and those who come to the Court in the years ahead may find it extremely difficult to overrule decisions which have been criticized as favoring those who need to be punished. There may be, indeed, some judicial whittling, but it would be uncommonly shocking if there were wholesale reversals.

It is always tempting to speculate, especially on the eve of a

9. *Cincinnati Law Review* 37, no. 4 (Fall 1968):721–722. Judge Friendly is U.S. Circuit Judge for the Second Circuit. In receiving a medal for outstanding public service on November 27, 1968, former New York Governor Thomas E. Dewey used the occasion to criticize the U.S. Supreme Court for its decisions which have resulted in "artificial restraints that tie up the courts and protect the guilty." He is quoted as having said that we could get along just as well if the Fifth Amendment were repealed. *New York Times*, November 28, 1968, p. 57.

10. 277 U.S., 470.

"new" Court. Restraint must overcome temptation, however, except for a brief commentary on a few of the directions the Warren Court has taken in giving status to the right to privacy.

It should be fairly safe to assume that the exclusionary rule will be applied in all courts even with the limitations prescribed in the 1968 omnibus crime act. Even though some states maintained variations of its opposite for some time, the practice before the state courts seems to follow the exclusionary rule in recent years, sufficiently so that it may now have a firm basis for the future. It is difficult to imagine that prudent and fair-minded men would accept the former scheme with such obviously different rules of evidence in federal and state courts. Judge Friendly's amendment might play havoc with the present exclusionary rule, among other things, but one may be optimistic and trust that most of his words will not become the law of the land.[11]

In the opinion in *Griswold*, Justice Douglas summarized the application of the Bill of Rights to the Fourteenth Amendment and used the label "zones of privacy." Justice Black, of course, denies any place for "privacy" as a fundamental right, but the majority has put its stamp of approval on the right to privacy. The only new aspect of privacy and the incorporation of the Bill of Rights into the Fourteenth Amendment was the label given. On the other hand, Douglas refers to prior decisions which created the zones.[12]

11. On December 1, 1968, the Philadelphia Police Department issued a series of pamphlets designed to help the police in the conduct of their assignments and to see that many situations they face have two sides. The authors of the series stated that the "strictures" of decisions of the U.S. Supreme Court have allowed relatively few guilty people to go free when compared to the mass who have not or the "larger number" of criminals who are never caught. *New York Times*, December 1, 1968, p. 40.

12. Critics may also agree with Judge Biggs' comment in *Ettore* v. *Philco Broadcasting Corp.*, 229 F 2d 481 (1956). "The state of the law is still that of a haystack in a hurricane. . . . We read of the right of privacy, of invasion of property rights, of breach of contract, of equitable servitude, of unfair competition; and there are even suggestions of unjust enrichment" (485).

Justice Goldberg's introduction of the Ninth Amendment as having some bearing on rights is novel, but as he put it:

> The Ninth Amendment to the Constitution may be regarded by some as a recent discovery . . . , but since 1791 it has been a basic part of the Constitution which we are sworn to uphold . . . nor am I turning somersaults with history in arguing that the Ninth Amendment is relevant in a case dealing with a *State's* infringement of a fundamental right. . . . Nor do I mean to state that the Ninth Amendment constitutes an independent source of rights protected from infringement by either the states or the Federal Government. Rather, the Ninth Amendment shows a belief of the Constitution's authors that fundamental rights exist that are not expressly enumerated in the first eight amendments and an intent that the list of rights included there not be deemed exhaustive.[13]

Undoubtedly the opinions in *Griswold* indicate that the future development of a right to privacy is still subject to "continuing probing and refinement."[14]

The post-Warren Court and its successors will be faced with the troublesome and controversial "right" to be silent. The *Miranda* decision supports that right to the extent that an accused must be told that he is not obliged to speak and he will not be penalized if he remains silent. Judge Friendly's amendment would open the door wide to interrogations and require answers, written and oral. It would compel anyone under subpoena to produce anything requested. Comment could be made freely in a trial about the silence of an accused. If the Friendly amendment had prevailed in 1964, for example, the Florida legislative committee would have had a field day with Mr. Gibson's list of members of the National Association for the Advancement of Colored People.

13. *Griswold* v. *Connecticut*, 381 U.S., 491, 492, 493.

14. Robert G. Dixon, Jr., "The Griswold Penumbra: Constitutional Charter for an Expanded Law of Privacy?", *Michigan Law Review* 64, no. 2 (December 1965): 197, 218, 206. Four other articles in the same issue consider the right to privacy from varying points of view.

In due course the constitutionality of the 1968 crime act will be tested before the U.S. Supreme Court. Title III which authorizes wiretapping and other forms of eavesdropping will collide with decisions such as *Berger* and *Katz*. If these and related decisions fall, then there is strong support for the claims of the critics of the crime act that Congress has given the police a power superior to the power of the courts to deny any claim of superiority. If the post-Warren Court reverses because of the criticisms directed against those decisions, it presumably would do so to stop the attacks and help its own preservation. But if it did so, would it not be open to an invitation to encourage even more curbs on its judicial authority? It should be remembered that eavesdropping has been sanctioned under some conditions and the concerns may arise only if the authority under Title III is abused.

To those whose chief concern about privacy is not involvement for wrongdoing, but only the desire to be let alone, the future may be no worse than the present. Religious pamphleteers may abound and annoying solicitors may frequent one's doorstep and ring his doorbell, but he may be spared other hawksters and peddlers if local governing bodies can be convinced of the desire for privacy. Sound-amplifying devices can be controlled somewhat. But it may be difficult to keep the inquiring reporter away or deny him his newsworthy bit however much it may invade privacy. One cannot expect much privacy in politics or public office; he can only hope for fairness and accuracy.

We can be less hopeful if we accept the pessimism voiced by Justice Douglas or the evidence given in the hearings before the subcommittees of the 89th Congress on privacy invasions.[15] But however distressing are those views and the

15. See his opinion in *Osborn*, 385 U.S. 323. Also, U.S. Senate, Hearings on Invasion of Privacy by Government Agencies Before the Subcommittee on Administrative Practices and Procedure of the Senate Committee on the Judiciary, 89th Cong., 1st sess., 1965; and U.S. House of Representatives, Hearings on Invasion of Privacy Before a Subcommittee of the House Government Operations Committee, 89th Cong., 1st sess., 1965.

facts presented, one can hope that those who will make the rules and those who will occupy the chairs in the halls of justice will be men of reason and good will and will have a respect for the dignity of man.[16] The ordinary man must put his trust in others even though some will abuse that trust. Yet, those who abuse it should be mindful that even the ordinary man is not without some resources to carry out his responsibilities as a citizen and prevent or correct any erosion of his rights.

Perhaps it will be recognized that when the rights and freedoms of the worst among us are respected, then, too, the rights and freedoms of the best will also be observed.

16. Warren Earl Burger of Minnesota succeeded Earl Warren as Chief Justice of the United States on June 23, 1969. At the time President Nixon announced his appointment on May 21, 1969, he was serving as judge on the U.S. Court of Appeals for the District of Columbia.

The Senate Judiciary Committee devoted less than two hours in interrogating Judge Burger and seventy-two seconds to give unanimous support of his nomination to the Senate. The Senate confirmed the appointment after three hours of debate with three dissenting votes.

There was little Senate inquiry into Judge Burger's judicial philosophy. While on the Court of Appeals he had frequently dissented in cases relating to the U.S. Supreme Court right-to-counsel decisions and rulings on unwarranted delays in taking arrested persons before magistrates. In one case where the majority applied the *Mallory* rule he charged that such rulings abandoned the balance between the rights of the individual and the protection of the public interest.

For a résumé of Judge Burger's opinions in 1968 and early 1969 see *Congressional Quarterly* 27, no. 22 (May 30, 1969):841–844.

Appendix

As indicated elsewhere, the article, "The Right to Privacy," by Samuel D. Warren and Louis D. Brandeis has been the source and reference for many court decisions and opinions about a right to privacy. It has been quoted many times. In determining privacy as a *right* it may be the most influential article ever published.

The article originally appeared in *Harvard Law Review* 4 (December 15, 1890). It is reprinted here in its entirety except for the notes.

The generally accepted view is that the article had its origins in the thoughts and anger of Warren, resulting from what he considered unwarranted invasions of personal and family privacy. Mrs. Warren was a member of a socially prominent Boston family and enjoyed lavishly done entertainment. At least one newspaper reported some of these events and on occasion related what the Warrens considered to be very personal and even embarrassing observations.

Brandeis was Warren's law partner. In later life Brandeis let it be known that while he worked with Warren on the article, it was with Warren's urging that he did so. In any event, it is a famous piece of writing. Its ideas and arguments helped form the basis of hundreds of lawsuits.

The Right to Privacy

by Samuel D. Warren and Louis D. Brandeis

That the individual shall have full protection in person and in property is a principle as old as the common law; but it has been found necessary from time to time to define anew the exact nature and extent of such protection. Political, social, and economic changes entail the recognition of new rights, and the common law, in its eternal youth, grows to meet the demands of society. Thus, in very early times, the law gave a remedy only for physical interference with life and property, for trespasses *vi et armis*. Then the "right to life" served only to protect the subject from battery in it various forms; liberty meant freedom from actual restraint; and the right to property secured to the individual his lands and his cattle. Later, there came a recognition of man's spiritual nature, of his feelings and his intellect. Gradually the scope of these legal rights broadened; and now the right to life has come to mean the right to enjoy life,—the right to be let alone; the right to liberty secures the exercise of extensive civil privileges; and the term "property" has grown to comprise every form of possession—intangible, as well as tangible.

Thus, with the recognition of the legal value of sensations, the protection against actual bodily injury was extended to prohibit mere attempts to do such injury; that is, the putting another in fear of such injury. From the action of battery grew that of assault. Much later there came a qualified protection of the individual against offensive noises and odors, against dust and smoke, and excessive vibration. The law of nuisance was developed. So regard for human emotions soon extended the scope of personal immunity beyond the body of the individual. His reputation, the standing among his fellow-men, was considered, and the law of slander and libel arose. Man's family relations became a part of the legal conception of his life, and the alienation of a wife's affections was held remediable. Occasionally the law halted,—as in its refusal to recognize the intrusion by seduction upon the honor of the family. But even here the demands of society were met. A mean fiction, the action *per quod servitium amisit*, was resorted to, and by allowing damages for injury to the parents' feelings, an adequate remedy was ordinarily afforded. Similar to the expansion of the right to life was the growth of the legal conception of property. From corporeal property arose the incorporeal rights issuing out of it; and then there opened the wide realm of intangible property, in the products and processes of the mind, as works of literature and art, goodwill, trade secrets, and trademarks.

This development of the law was inevitable. The intense intellectual and emotional life, and the heightening of sensations which came with the advance of civilization, made it clear to men that only a part of the pain, pleasure, and profit of life lay in physical things. Thoughts, emotions, and sensations demanded legal recognition, and the beautiful capacity for growth which characterizes the common law enabled the judges to afford the requisite protection, without the interposition of the legislature.

Recent inventions and business methods call attention to the next step which must be taken for the protection of the person, and for securing to the individual what Judge Cooley calls the right "to be let alone." Instantaneous photographs and newspaper enterprise have invaded the sacred precincts of private and domestic life; and numerous mechanical devices threaten to make good the prediction that "what is whispered in the closet shall be proclaimed from the house-tops." For years there has been a feeling that the law must afford some remedy for the unauthorized circulation of portraits of private persons; and the evil of the invasion of

privacy by the newspapers, long keenly felt, has been but
recently discussed by an able writer. The alleged facts of a
somewhat notorious case brought before an inferior tribunal
in New York a few months ago, directly involved the consideration of the right of circulating portraits; and the question
whether our law will recognize and protect the right to privacy
in this and in other respects must soon come before our
courts for consideration.

Of the desirability—indeed of the necessity—of some such
protection, there can, it is believed, be no doubt. The press is
overstepping in every direction the obvious bounds of propriety and of decency. Gossip is no longer the resource of the
idle and of the vicious, but has become a trade, which is
pursued with industry as well as effrontery. To satisfy a prurient taste the details of sexual relations are spread broadcast
in the columns of the daily papers. To occupy the indolent,
column upon column is filled with idle gossip, which can only
be procured by intrusion upon the domestic circle. The inten-
sity and complexity of life, attendant upon advancing civilization, have rendered necessary some retreat from the
world, and man, under the refining influence of culture, has
become more sensitive to publicity, so that solitude and privacy
have become more essential to the individual; but modern
enterprise and invention have, through invasions upon his
privacy, subjected him to mental pain and distress, far greater
than could be inflicted by mere bodily injury. Nor is the harm
wrought by such invasions confined to the suffering of those
who may be made the subjects of journalistic or other enterprise. In this, as in other branches of commerce, the supply
creates the demand. Each crop of unseemly gossip, thus
harvested, becomes the seed of more, and, in direct propor-
tion to its circulation, results in a lowering of social standards
and of morality. Even gossip apparently harmless, when
widely and persistently circulated, is potent for evil. It both
belittles and perverts. It belittles by inverting the relative
importance of things, thus dwarfing the thoughts and aspi-
rations of a people. When personal gossip attains the dignity
of print, and crowds the space available for matters of real

interest to the community, what wonder that the ignorant and thoughtless mistake its relative importance. Easy of comprehension, appealing to that weak side of human nature which is never wholly cast down by the misfortunes and frailties of our neighbors, no one can be surprised that it usurps the place of interest in brains capable of other things. Triviality destroys at once robustness of thought and delicacy of feeling. No enthusiasm can flourish, no generous impulse can survive under its blighting influence.

It is our purpose to consider whether the existing law affords a principle which can properly be invoked to protect the privacy of the individual; and, if it does, what the nature and extent of such protection is.

Owing to the nature of the instruments by which privacy is invaded, the injury inflicted bears a superficial resemblance to the wrongs dealt with by the law of slander and of libel, while a legal remedy for such injury seems to involve the treatment of mere wounded feelings, as a substantive cause of action. The principle on which the law of defamation rests, covers, however, a radically different class of effects from those for which attention is now asked. It deals only with damage to reputation, with the injury done to the individual in his external relations to the community, by lowering him in the estimation of his fellows. The matter published of him, however widely circulated, and however unsuited to publicity, must, in order to be actionable, have a direct tendency to injure him in his intercourse with others, and even if in writing or in print, must subject him to the hatred, ridicule, or contempt of his fellowmen,—the effect of the publication upon his estimate of himself and upon his own feelings not forming an essential element in the cause of action. In short, the wrongs and correlative rights recognized by the law of slander and libel are in their nature material rather than spiritual. That branch of the law simply extends the protection surrounding physical property to certain of the conditions necessary or helpful to worldly prosperity. On the other hand, our law recognizes no principle upon which compensation can be granted for mere injury to the feelings. However painful the. mental effects upon another of an act, though purely wanton or even malicious, yet if the act itself is otherwise lawful, the suffering inflicted is *damnum absque injuria*. Injury of feelings may indeed be taken account of in ascertaining the amount of damages when attending what is recognized as a legal injury; but our system, unlike the Roman law, does not afford a remedy even for mental suffering which results from mere contumely and insult, from an intentional and unwarranted violation of the "honor" of another.

It is not however necessary, in order to sustain the view that the common law recognizes and upholds a principle applicable to cases of invasion of privacy, to invoke the analogy, which is but superficial, to injuries sustained, either by an attack upon reputation or by what the civilians called a violation of honor; for the legal doctrines relating to infractions of what is ordinarily termed the common-law right to intellectual and artistic property are, it is believed, but instances and applications of a general right to privacy, which properly understood afford a remedy for the evils under consideration.

The common law secures to each individual the right of determining, ordinarily, to what extent his thoughts, sentiments, and emotions shall be communicated to others. Under our system of government, he can never be compelled to express them (except when upon the witness-stand); and even if he has chosen to give them expression, he generally retains the power to fix the limits of the publicity which shall be given them. The existence of this right does not depend upon the particular method of expression adopted. It is immaterial whether it be by word or by signs, in painting, by sculpture, or in music. Neither does the existence of the right depend upon the nature or value of the thought or emotion, nor upon the excellence of the means of expression. The same protection is accorded to a casual letter or an entry in a diary and to the most valuable poem or essay, to a botch or daub and to a masterpiece. In every such case the individual is entitled to decide whether that which is his shall be given to the public. No other has the right to publish his productions

in any form, without his consent. This right is wholly independent of the material on which, or the means by which,
the thought, sentiment, or emotion is expressed. It may exist
independently of any corporeal being, as in words spoken, a
song sung, a drama acted. Or if expressed on any material,
as a poem in writing, the author may have parted with the
paper, without forfeiting any proprietary right in the composition itself. The right is lost only when the author himself
communicates his production to the public,—in other words,
publishes it. It is entirely independent of the copyright laws,
and their extension into the domain of art. The aim of those
statutes is to secure to the author, composer, or artist the entire
profits arising from publication; but the common-law protection enables him to control absolutely the act of publication,
and in the exercise of his own discretion, to decide whether
there shall be any publication at all. The statutory right is
of no value, *unless* there is a publication; the common-law
right is lost *as soon as* there is a publication.

What is the nature, the basis, of this right to prevent the
publication of manuscripts or works of art? It is stated to be
the enforcement of a right of property; and no difficulty
arises in accepting this view, so long as we have only to deal
with the reproduction of literary and artistic compositions.
They certainly possess many of the attributes of ordinary
property: they are transferable; they have a value; and
publication or reproduction is a use by which that value is
realized. But where the value of the production is found not in
the right to take the profits arising from publication, but in
the peace of mind or the relief afforded by the ability to
prevent any publication at all, it is difficult to regard the right
as one of property, in the common acceptation of that term.
A man records in a letter to his son, or in his diary, that he
did not dine with his wife on a certain day. No one into
whose hands those papers fall could publish them to the world,
even if possession of the documents had been obtained rightfully; and the prohibition would not be confined to the
publication of a copy of the letter itself, or of the diary entry;
the restraint extends also to a publication of the contents.

What is the thing which is protected? Surely, not the intellectual act of recording the fact that the husband did not dine
with his wife, but that fact itself. It is not the intellectual
product, but the domestic occurrence. A man writes a dozen
letters to different people. No person would be permitted to
publish a list of the letters written. If the letters or the contents
of the diary were protected as literary compositions, the scope
of the protection afforded should be the same secured to a
published writing under the copyright law. But the copyright
law would not prevent an enumeration of the letters, or the
publication of some of the facts contained therein. The
copyright of a series of paintings or etchings would prevent
a reproduction of the paintings as pictures; but it would not
prevent a publication of a list or even a description of them.
Yet in the famous case of Prince Albert v. Strange, the court
held that the common-law rule prohibited not merely the
reproduction of the etchings which the plaintiff and Queen
Victoria had made for their own pleasure, but also, "the
publishing (at least by printing or writing), though not by
copy or resemblance, a description of them, whether more or
less limited or summary, whether in the form of a catalog or
otherwise." Likewise, an unpublished collection of news
possessing no element of a literary nature is protected from
piracy.

That this protection cannot rest upon the right to literary
or artistic property in any exact sense, appears the more
clearly when the subject-matter for which protection is
invoked is not even in the form of intellectual property, but
has the attributes of ordinary tangible property. Suppose a
man has a collection of gems or curiosities which he keeps
private: it would hardly be contended that any person could
publish a catalogue of them, and yet the articles enumerated
are certainly not intellectual property in the legal sense, any
more than a collection of stoves or of chairs.

The belief that the idea of property in its narrow sense was
the basis of the protection of unpublished manuscripts led an
able court to refuse, in several cases, injunctions against the
publication of private letters, on the ground that "letters not

possessing the attributes of literary compositions are not property entitled to protection;" and that it was "evident the plaintiff could not have considered the letters as of any value whatever as literary productions, for a letter cannot be considered of value to the author which he never would consent to have published." But these decisions have not been followed, and it may now be considered settled that the protection afforded by the common law to the author of any writing is entirely independent of its pecuniary value, its intrinsic merits, or of any intention to publish the same, and, of course, also, wholly independent of the material, if any, upon which, or the mode in which, the thought or sentiment was expressed.

Although the courts have asserted that they rested their decisions on the narrow grounds of protection to property, yet there are recognitions of a more liberal doctrine. Thus in the case of Prince Albert *v.* Strange, already referred to, the opinions both of the Vice-Chancellor and of the Lord Chancellor, on appeal, show a more or less clearly defined perception of a principle broader than those which were mainly discussed, and on which they both placed their chief reliance. Vice-Chancellor Knight Bruce referred to publishing of a man that he had "written to particular persons or on particular subjects" as an instance of possibly injurious disclosures as to private matters, that the courts would in a proper case prevent; yet it is difficult to perceive how, in such a case, any right of property, in the narrow sense, would be drawn in question, or why, if such a publication would be restrained when it threatened to expose the victim not merely to sarcasm, but to ruin, it should not equally be enjoined, if it threatened to embitter his life. To deprive a man of the potential profits to be realized by publishing a catalogue of his gems cannot *per se* be a wrong to him. The possibility of future profits is not a right of property which the law ordinarily recognizes; it must, therefore, be an infraction of other rights which constitutes the wrongful act, and that infraction is equally wrongful, whether its results are to forestall the profits that the individual himself might secure by giving the matter a publicity obnoxious to him, or to gain an advantage at the expense of his mental pain and suffering. If the fiction of property in a narrow sense must be preserved, it is still true that the end accomplished by the gossip-monger is attained by the use of that which is another's, the facts relating to his private life, which he has seen fit to keep private. Lord Cottenham stated that a man "is entitled to be protected in the exclusive use and enjoyment of that which is exclusively his," and cited with approval the opinion of Lord Eldon, as reported in a manuscript note of the case of Wyatt *v.* Wilson, in 1820, respecting an engraving of George the Third during his illness, to the effect that "if one of the late king's physicians had kept a diary of what he heard and saw, the court would not, in the king's lifetime, have permitted him to print and publish it;" and Lord Cottenham declared, in respect to the acts of the defendants in the case before him, that "privacy is the right invaded." But if privacy is once recognized as a right entitled to legal protection, the interposition of the courts cannot depend on the particular nature of the injuries resulting.

These considerations lead to the conclusion that the protection afforded to thoughts, sentiments, and emotions, expressed through the medium of writing or of the arts, so far as it consists in preventing publication, is merely an instance of the enforcement of the more general right of the individual to be let alone. It is like the right not to be assaulted or beaten, the right not to be imprisoned, the right not to be maliciously prosecuted, the right not to be defamed. In each of these rights, as indeed in all other rights recognized by the law, there inheres the quality of being owned or possessed— and (as that is the disguishing attribute of property) there may be some propriety in speaking of those rights as property. But, obviously, they bear little resemblance to what is ordinarily comprehended under that term. The principle which protects personal writings and all other personal productions, not against theft and physical appropriation but against publication in any form, is in reality not the principle of private property, but that of an inviolate personality.

If we are correct in this conclusion, the existing law affords a principle which may be invoked to protect the privacy of the individual from invasion either by the too enterprising press, the photographer, or the possessor of any other modern device for recording or reproducing scenes or sounds. For the protection afforded is not confined by the authorities to those cases where any particular medium or form of expression has been adopted, nor to products of the intellect. The same protection is afforded to emotions and sensations expressed in a musical composition or other work of art as to a literary composition; and words spoken, a pantomime acted, a sonata performed, is no less entitled to protection than if each had been reduced to writing. The circumstance that a thought or emotion has been recorded in a permanent form renders its identification easier, and hence may be important from the point of view of evidence, but it has no significance as a matter of substantive right. If, then, the decisions indicate a general right to privacy for thoughts, emotions, and sensations, these should receive the same protection, whether expressed in writing, or in conduct, in conversation, in attitudes, or in facial expression.

It may be urged that a distinction should be taken between the deliberate expression of thoughts and emotions in literary or artistic compositions and the casual and often involuntary expression given to them in the ordinary conduct of life. In other words, it may be contended that the protection afforded is granted to the conscious products of labor, perhaps as an encouragement to effort. This contention, however plausible, has, in fact, little to recommend it. If the amount of labor involved be adopted as the test, we might well find that the effort to conduct one's self properly in business and in domestic relations had been far greater than that involved in painting a picture or writing a book; one would find that it was far easier to express lofty sentiments in a diary than in the conduct of a noble life. If the test of deliberateness of the act be adopted, much casual correspondence which is now accorded full protection would be excluded from the beneficent operation of existing rules. After the decisions denying the distinction attempted to be made between those literary productions which it was intended to publish and those which it was not, all considerations of the amount of labor involved, the degree of deliberation, the value of the product, and the intention of publishing must be abandoned, and no basis is discerned upon which the right to restrain publication and reproduction of such so-called literary and artistic works can be rested, except the right to privacy, as a part of the more general right to the immunity of the person,—the right to one's personality.

It should be stated that, in some instances where protection has been afforded against wrongful publication, the jurisdiction has been asserted, not on the ground of property, or at least not wholly on that ground but upon the ground of an alleged breach of an implied contract or of a trust of confidence.

Thus, in Abernethy v. Hutchinson, 3 L.J. Ch. 209 (1825), where the plaintiff, a distinguished surgeon, sought to restrain the publication in the "Lancet" of unpublished lectures which he had delivered at St. Bartholomew's Hospital in London, Lord Eldon doubted whether there could be property in lectures which had not been reduced to writing, but granted the injunction on the ground of breach of confidence, holding "that when persons were admitted as pupils or otherwise, to hear these lectures, although they were orally delivered, and although the parties might go to the extent, if they were able to do so, of putting down the whole by means of short-hand, yet they could do that only for the purposes of their own information, and could not publish, for profit, that which they had not obtained the right of selling."

In Prince Albert v. Strange, 1 McN. & G. 25 (1849), Lord Cottenham, on appeal, while recognizing a right of property in the etchings which of itself would justify the issuance of the injunction, stated, after discussing the evidence, that he was bound to assume that the possession of the etchings by the defendant had "its foundations in a breach of trust, confidence, or contract," and that upon such ground also the plaintiff's title to the injunction was fully sustained.

In Tuck v. Priester, 19 Q.B.D. 639 (1887), the plaintiffs were owners of a picture, and employed the defendant to make a certain number of copies. He did so, and made also a number of other copies for himself, and offered them for sale in England at a lower price. Subsequently, the plaintiffs registered their copyright in the picture, and then brought suit for an injunction and damages. The Lords Justices differed as to the application of the copyright acts to the case, but held unanimously that independently of those acts, the plaintiffs were entitled to an injunction and damages for breach of contract.

In Pollard v. Photographic Co., 40 Ch. Div. 345 (1888), a photographer who had taken a lady's photograph under the ordinary circumstances was restrained from exhibiting it, and also from selling copies of it, on the ground that it was a breach of an implied term in the contract, and also that it was a breach of confidence. Mr. Justice North interjected in the argument of the plaintiff's counsel the inquiry: "Do you dispute that if the negative likeness were taken on the sly, the person who took it might exhibit copies?" and counsel for the plaintiff answered: "In that case there would be no trust or consideration to support a contract." Later, the defendant's counsel argued that "a person has no property in his own features; short of doing what is libellous or otherwise illegal, there is no restriction on the photographer's using his negative." But the court, while expressly finding a breach of contract and of trust sufficient to justify its interposition, still seems to have felt the necessity of resting the decision also upon a right of property, in order to bring it within the line of those cases which were relied upon as precedents.

This process of implying a term in a contract, or of implying a trust (particularly where the contract is written, and where there is no established usage or custom), is nothing more nor less than a judicial declaration that public morality, private justice, and general convenience demand the recognition of

such a rule, and that the publication under similar circumstances would be considered an intolerable abuse. So long
as these circumstances happen to present a contract upon
which such a term can be engrafted by the judicial mind,
or to supply relations upon which a trust or confidence can
be erected, there may be no objection to working out the
desired protection through the doctrines of contract or of
trust. But the court can hardly stop there. The narrower
doctrine may have satisfied the demands of society at a time
when the abuse to be guarded against could rarely have arisen
without violating a contract or a special confidence; but now
that modern devices afford abundant opportunities for the
perpetration of such wrongs without any participation by
the injured party, the protection granted by the law must
be placed upon a broader foundation. While, for instance,
the state of the photographic art was such that one's picture
could seldom be taken without his consciously "sitting" for
the purpose, the law of contract or of trust might afford the
prudent man sufficient safeguards against the improper
circulation of his portrait; but since the latest advances in
photographic art have rendered it possible to take pictures
surreptitiously, the doctrines of contract and of trust are
inadequate to support the required protection, and the law
of tort must be resorted to. The right of property in its widest
sense, including all possession, including all rights and privileges, and hence embracing the right to an inviolate personality, affords alone that broad basis upon which the protection
which the individual demands can be rested.

Thus, the courts, in searching for some principle upon
which the publication of private letters could be enjoined,
naturally came upon the ideas of a breach of confidence, and
of an implied contract; but it required little consideration to
discern that this doctrine could not afford all the protection
required, since it would not support the court in granting a
remedy against a stranger; and so the theory of property
in the contents of letters was adopted. Indeed, it is difficult
to conceive on what theory of the law the casual recipient
of a letter, who proceeds to publish it, is guilty of a breach

of contract, express or implied, or of any breach of trust, in the ordinary acceptation of that term. Suppose a letter has been addressed to him without his solicitation. He opens it, and reads. Surely, he has not made any contract; he has not accepted any trust. He cannot, by opening and reading the letter, have come under any obligation save what the law declares; and, however expressed, that obligation is simply to observe the legal right of the sender, whatever it may be, and whether it be called his right of property in the contents of the letter, or his right to privacy.

A similar groping for the principle upon which a wrongful publication can be enjoined is found in the law of trade secrets. There, injunctions have generally been granted on the theory of a breach of contract, or of an abuse of confidence. It would, of course, rarely happen that any one would be in the possession of a secret unless confidence had been reposed in him. But can it be supposed that the court would hesitate to grant relief against one who had obtained his knowledge by an ordinary trespass,—for instance, by wrongfully looking into a book in which the secret was recorded, or by eavesdropping? Indeed, in Yovatt *v.* Winyard, 1 J. & W. 394 (1820), where an injunction was granted against making any use of or communicating certain recipes for veterinary medicine, it appeared that the defendant, while in the plaintiff's employ, had surreptitiously got access to his book of recipes, and copied them. Lord Eldon "granted the injunction, upon the gound of there having been a breach of trust and confidence;" but it would seem to be difficult to draw any sound legal distinction between such a case and one where a mere stranger wrongfully obtained access to the book.

We must therefore conclude that the rights, so protected, whatever their exact nature, are not rights arising from contract or from special trust, but are rights as against the world; and, as above stated, the principle which has been applied to protect these rights is in reality not the principle of private property, unless that word be used in an extended and unusual sense. The principle which protects personal writings and any other productions of the intellect or of the emotions, is the right to privacy and the law has no new principle to formulate when it extends this protection to the personal appearance, sayings, acts, and to personal relations, domestic or otherwise.

If the invasion of privacy constitutes a legal *injuria*, the elements for demanding redress exist, since already the value of mental suffering, caused by an act wrongful in itself, is recognized as a basis for compensation.

The right of one who has remained a private individual, to prevent his public portraiture, presents the simplest case for such extension; the right to protect one's self from pen portraiture, from a discussion by the press of one's private affairs, would be a more important and far-reaching one. If casual and unimportant statements in a letter, if handiwork, however inartistic and valueless, if possessions of all sorts are protected not only against reproduction, but against description and enumeration, how much more should the acts and sayings of a man in his social and domestic relations be guarded from ruthless publicity. If you may not reproduce a woman's face photographically without her consent, how much less should be tolerated the reproduction of her face, her form, and her actions, by graphic descriptions colored to suit a gross and depraved imagination.

The right to privacy, limited as such right must necessarily be, has already found expression in the law of France.

It remains to consider what are the limitations of this right to privacy, and what remedies may be granted for the enforcement of the right. To determine in advance of experience the exact line at which the dignity and convenience of the individual must yield to the demands of the public welfare or of private justice would be a difficult task; but the more general rules are furnished by the legal analogies already developed in the law of slander and libel, and in the law of literary and artistic property.

1. The right to privacy does not prohibit any publication of matter which is of public or general interest.

In determining the scope of this rule, aid would be afforded by the analogy, in the law of libel and slander, of cases which deal with the qualified privilege of comment and criticism on matters of public and general interest. There are of course difficulties in applying such a rule; but they are inherent in the subject-matter, and are certainly no greater than those which exist in many other branches of the law,—for instance, in that large class of cases in which the reasonableness or unreasonableness of an act is made the test of liability. The design of the law must be to protect those persons with whose affairs the community has no legitimate concern, from being dragged into an undesirable and undesired publicity and to protect all persons, whatsoever; their position or station, from having matters which they may properly prefer to keep private, made public against their will. It is the unwarranted invasion of individual privacy which is reprehended, and to be, so far as possible, prevented. The distinction, however, noted in the above statement is obvious and fundamental. There are persons who may reasonably claim as a right, protection from the notoriety entailed by being made the victims of journalistic enterprise. There are others who, in varying degrees, have renounced the right to live their lives screened from public observation. Matters which men of the first class may justly contend, concern themselves alone, may in those of the second be the subject of legitimate interest to their fellow-citizens. Peculiarities of manner and person, which in the ordinary individual should be free from comment, may acquire a public importance, if found in a candidate for political office. Some further discrimination is necessary, therefore, than to class facts or deeds as public or private according to a standard to be applied to the fact or deed *per se*. To publish of a modest and retiring individual that he suffers from an impediment in his speech or that he cannot spell correctly, is an unwarranted, if not an unexampled, infringement of his rights, while to state and comment on the same characteristics found in a would-be congressman would not be regarded as beyond the pale of propriety.

The general object in view is to protect the privacy of

private life, and to whatever degree and in whatever connection a man's life has ceased to be private, before the publication under consideration has been made, to that extent the protection is to be withdrawn. Since, then, the propriety of publishing the very same facts may depend wholly upon the person concerning whom they are published, no fixed formula can be used to prohibit obnoxious publications. Any rule of liability adopted must have in it an elasticity which shall take account of the varying circumstances of each case,—a necessity which unfortunately renders such a doctrine not only more difficult of application, but also to a certain extent uncertain in its operation and easily rendered abortive. Besides, it is only the more flagrant breaches of decency and propriety that could in practice be reached, and it is not perhaps desirable even to attempt to repress everything which the nicest taste and keenest sense of the respect due to private life would condemn.

In general, then, the matters of which the publication should be repressed may be described as those which concern the private life, habits, acts, and relations of an individual, and have no legitimate connection with his fitness for a public office which he seeks or for which he is suggested, or for any public or quasi public position which he seeks or for which he is suggested, and have no legitimate relation to or bearing upon any act done by him in a public or quasi public capacity. The foregoing is not designed as a wholly accurate or exhaustive definition, since that which must ultimately in a vast number of cases become a question of individual judgment and opinion is incapable of such definition; but it is an attempt to indicate broadly the class of matters referred to. Some things all men alike are entitled to keep from popular curiosity, whether in public life or not, while others are only private because the persons concerned have not assumed a position which makes their doings legitimate matters of public investigation.

2. The right to privacy does not prohibit the communication of any matter, though in its nature private, when the publication is made under circumstances which would render

it a privileged communication according to the law of slander and libel.

Under this rule, the right to privacy is not invaded by any publication made in a court of justice, in legislative bodies, or the committees of those bodies; in municipal assemblies, or the committees of such assemblies, or practically by any communication made in any other public body, municipal or parochial, or in any body quasi public, like the large voluntary associations formed for almost every purpose of benevolence, business, or other general interest; and (at least in many jurisdictions) reports of any such proceedings would in some measure be accorded a like privilege. Nor would the rule prohibit any publication made by one in the discharge of some public or private duty, whether legal or moral, or in the conduct of one's own affairs, in matters where his own interest is concerned.

3. The law would probably not grant any redress for the invasion of privacy by oral publication in the absence of special damage.

The same reasons exist for distinguishing between oral and written publications of private matters, as is afforded in the law of defamation by the restricted liability for slander as compared with the liability for libel. The injury resulting from such oral communications would ordinarily be so trifling that the law might well, in the interest of free speech, disregard it altogether.

4. The right to privacy ceases upon the publication of the facts by the individual, or with his consent.

This is but another application of the rule which has become familiar in the law of literary and artistic property. The cases there decided establish also what should be deemed a publication,—the important principle in this connection being that a private communication or circulation for a restricted purpose is not a publication within the meaning of the law.

5. The truth of the matter published does not afford a defence. Obviously this branch of the law should have no concern with the truth or falsehood of the matters published. It is not for injury to the individual's character that redress

or prevention is sought, but for injury to the right of privacy. For the former, the law of slander and libel provides perhaps a sufficient safeguard. The latter implies a right not merely to prevent inaccurate portrayal of private life, but to prevent its being depicted at all.

6. The absence of "malice" in the publisher does not afford a defence.—

Personal ill-will is not an ingredient of the offence, any more than in an ordinary case of trespass to person or to property. Such malice is never necessary to be shown in an action for libel or slander at common law, except in rebuttal of some defence, *e.g.*, that the occasion rendered the communication privileged, or, under the statutes in this State and elsewhere, that the statement complained of was true. The invasion of the privacy that is to be protected is equally complete and equally injurious, whether the motives by which the speaker or writer was actuated are, taken by themselves, culpable or not; just as the damage to character, and to some extent the tendency to provoke a breach of the peace, is equally the result of defamation without regard to the motives leading to its publication. Viewed as a wrong to the individual, this rule is the same pervading the whole law of torts, by which one is held responsible for his intentional acts, even though they are committed with no sinister intent; and viewed as a wrong to society, it is the same principle adopted in a large category of statutory offences.

The remedies for an invasion of the right of privacy are also suggested by those administered in the law of defamation, and in the law of literary and artistic property, namely:—

1. An action of tort for damages in all cases. Even in the absence of special damages, substantial compensation could be allowed for injury to feelings as in the action of slander and libel.

2. An injunction, in perhaps a very limited class of cases.

It would doubtless be desirable that the privacy of the individual should receive the added protection of the criminal law, but for this, legislation would be required. Perhaps it would be deemed proper to bring the criminal liability for such publication within narrower limits; but that the community has an interest in preventing such invasions of privacy, sufficiently strong to justify the introduction of such a remedy, cannot be doubted. Still, the protection of society must come mainly through a recognition of the rights of the individual. Each man is responsible for his own acts and omissions only. If he condones what he reprobates, with a weapon at hand equal to his defence, he is responsible for the results. If he resists, public opinion will rally to his support. Has he then such a weapon? It is believed that the common law provides him with one, forged in the slow fire of the centuries, and to-day fitly tempered to his hand. The common law has always recognized a man's house as his castle, impregnable, often, even to its own officers engaged in the execution of its commands. Shall the courts thus close the front entrance to constituted authority, and open wide the back door to idle or prurient curiosity?

Index to Court Cases